X27

A Spell from Laker

on cricket and cricketers
past and present

A Spell from Laker

on cricket and cricketers past and present

Jim Laker

Hamlyn
London · New York · Sydney · Toronto

Published by The Hamlyn Publishing Group Limited
London · New York · Sydney · Toronto
Astronaut House, Feltham, Middlesex, England
Copyright © Jim Laker 1979

ISBN 0 600 35259 5

Filmset in England by Photocomp Ltd., Birmingham
Printed in England by R. J. Acford Ltd., Chichester

Contents

The Oval

For reasons obvious to cricket lovers, Kennington Oval in South East London and Old Trafford in Manchester will forever hold pride of place for me amongst the many grounds not only of England but of the whole world. On the face of it there is nothing particularly attractive about either. Increasing costs of upkeep and maintenance have presented problems recently for the respective County committees responsible for their upkeep. Worcester with its cathedral and Capetown with its Table Mountain are beautiful grounds which are high on the lists of all cricketers, but I will still settle for the Oval, dominated by gasholders, and be happy at Old Trafford watching the Derbyshire hills disappear in the mist as the trains rattle through Warwick Road Station.

It is strange that a Yorkshireman should be attracted to the headquarters of Lancashire cricket and indeed look upon 5 acres of fertilised grass bang in the heart of South London's council tenements with such affection. I was not an impressionable teenager at the end of 1946 when I first walked through the Oval Long Room into the Professionals' dressing room. For five long and wearisome years in the Middle East I had endured the boredom of a soldier at a base depot, and had grown somewhat cynical before my years. The only relief from routine camp chores came my way through cricket and soccer when I had been privileged to encounter the best. Oddly I derived more pleasure in dispossessing Tom Finney in the six-yard box than finding a way through Dudley Nourse's defence with an off break. For all that, as I stripped off my khaki jacket, making sure that my sergeant's stripes were prominently displayed, I felt instantly that if I were to make a name in the game of cricket it would be done here at Kennington Oval. The simple fact was that I had to make a mark soon, thanks to those wasted years of war.

The 1946 season was just ending as I collected my grey pin-striped 'demob suit' and drew my first £6 weekly winter retainer from Surrey. A hard winter's practice at Alf Gover's Academy and there I was in my 26th year with as yet not a serious first-class match under my belt. It is interesting to reflect that at a comparable age Derek Underwood was very close to 1,000 first-class wickets! Despite my woeful lack of first-class experience, which hindered me for three or four years, I had been well and truly blooded in the very competitive Bradford League at the age of 15, and Middle East cricket had given me a number of notable international scalps. A quick breakthrough from Minor County cricket was vital, and it came in July after only half a dozen second eleven games. The final two months of the season far exceeded my wildest dreams. In those nine weeks I bowled nearly 600 overs and in the process captured 79 wickets at 17 apiece, headed the County bowling averages, was awarded my county cap and unbelievably was selected by MCC for the winter tour to the West Indies.

Surrey CCC in 1948, about to become a great side. *Left to right, back:* Herbert Strudwick, Arthur McIntyre, David Fletcher, Eric Bedser, Jack Parker, Alec Bedser, John McMahon, myself, Sandy Tait. *Front:* Eddie Watts, Tom Barling, Michael Barton, Stan Squires, Laurie Fishlock.
Preceding page: The Oval in my time: a full crowd for the Bank Holiday game with Notts.

Those two months told me that I could bowl and, more important, that with experience I could bowl for England. I also sensed that my adopted county was on the verge of becoming a very fine side. It was to take a year or two, during which time I saw the departure of those fine stalwarts, Alf Gover, Bob Gregory and Tom Barling, and mourned the tragic early death of Stan Squires. Laurie Fishlock and Jack Parker carried the flag and helped no end in the formation of a new generation of Surrey cricketers. They were led by Alec Bedser and Arthur McIntyre, two pre-war apprentices, with Bernie Constable, Tom Clark and David Fletcher close behind. From the depths of Surrey there appeared a young 17-year-old with a mop of red hair and all the confidence in the world. Little did I realise then that Tony Lock and I would together share so many glorious hours. Incredible stories reached the dressing room of a young writer in the Navy who was due shortly at Cambridge and would be available for Surrey. Peter May more than fulfilled everything that was predicted for him and truly became an all-time great. New players full of talent arrived at regular intervals boosting the professional staff to upwards of 22, and yet there was one alarming deficiency – a captain.

Since cricket was played there has always been a shortage of top-class leaders. Pre-war Surrey had come out better than most with such esteemed names as Percy Fender and Douglas Jardine but not until the seventh season after the war when Stuart Surridge was appointed (to the reluctance of some) did the county finally begin to achieve the success that so many of us felt was just round the corner.

It seems that Surrey were loath to accept the fact that Nigel Bennett had skippered the county in 1946 – it was several years before his photograph appeared in the committee room gallery. In fact it seems that Nigel himself was more than taken aback when the invitation reached him as he was enjoying his demob leave. He was unheard of in first-class cricket, or even in Minor County cricket, and how the appointment came about remained a complete mystery to the players themselves. However a widely accepted theory was that Surrey had intended offering the captaincy to Leo Bennett, a first-class club cricketer with county experience at Northampton, but through a misunderstanding the invitation arrived on Nigel's doorstep. He accepted with alacrity. I would not

Above left: Nigel Bennett, Surrey Captain in 1946, some thought by accident.
Above: The captain of 1947, Errol Holmes, a man who was jealous of the privileges of the amateur.
Right: A shot of me bowling in 1950, the year Surrey shared the championship with Lancashire, our first success since 1914.

attempt to describe some of the hair-raising predicaments that Nigel found himself in during 1946. I found him to be a thoroughly likeable fellow and enjoyed his company, but on the field he was like a fish out of water throughout the entire season. Players, and even more so, officials, breathed a huge sigh of relief when his term of office expired.

In complete contrast, and in the spirit of taking no further chances, Surrey persuaded their own pre-war amateur, 42-year-old E.R.T. Holmes, to take over in 1947. Not, I fancy, that he needed much persuasion. Perhaps I should have been grateful to Errol Holmes as it was he who brought me into the side and gave me a county cap after only a dozen games or so. Unhappily he epitomised the few points I despised in the amateur cricketer. He lived in a world completely divorced from those of us whose initials followed our name. He relished and thrived on his separate changing quarters and his different travel facilities. A severe dressing down came the way of no less a senior cricketer than Alf Gover, who had inadvertently, and on a solitary occasion, addressed him as 'Errol' instead of 'Mr Holmes'. He summarily dismissed Tom Barling from the Oval staff after 20 years service, and left that fine player in tears. His judgement of a cricketer was such that he told me on one occasion that John McMahon was potentially the finest bowler in the world. John, a dear friend of mine, often struggled to make the

Champions! The side in 1952, the first of Surrey's seven consecutive years as county champions. *Left to right, back:* David Fletcher, Tony Lock, John McMahon, Eric Bedser, myself, Geoff Whittaker, Bernard Constable. *Front:* Alec Bedser, Laurie Fishlock, Stuart Surridge, Jack Parker, Arthur McIntyre.

Surrey side bowling left-hand off breaks, and on hearing this praise confided to me that he had clean bowled Errol at least half a dozen times in the nets that morning. Perhaps Errol Holmes' most outrageous suggestion to brighten the game was that 20 runs instead of six should be awarded for each shot that cleared the boundary. Malcolm Nash would have loved his figures to be 0 for 120 after his over at Sobers!

Like many of his amateur colleagues, 'E.R.T.' was a courageous batsman and on a hard flat pitch was a glorious stroke player. He had developed the Malvern drive better than any Malverian. He completed a brilliant double century at Chesterfield with a straight six over the pavilion off paceman Bill Copson and in 1947 hammered the Notts attack for a hundred before lunch. It became a different story if the ball swung in or spun off the pitch. I recall becoming almost excited bowling to Errol in a Surrey trial match, where the gap between bat and pad was so enormous that I could pick out Arthur McIntyre crouching behind the wicket. His appearances in the following year of 1948 became more spasmodic and he negotiated his replacement in the shape of another old Oxford blue, M.R. Barton. As a player Mike had a wonderful start, collecting three hundreds in his first four games, and he was well worth his place when he captained the county through to the end of 1951.

I can never recall any of my colleagues uttering an unkind word about Michael Barton. He was quiet, reserved and had a subtle sense of humour. His discipline was well organised and conducted in a manner which never offended. He took me to task on a couple of occasions, quietly and privately, and proved most conclusively that I had been in the wrong. As a captain, however, he was utterly predictable, seldom took a chance and lacked that flair that makes all the difference. He ruled by the clock, and I knew that if we lost the toss I should come on to bowl at 12.10 and remain at one end until 1 pm when the quicker bowlers would return until lunch. His solitary day of panic happened at Leicester, when he forgot to take his wrist watch on the field and the pavilion clock stopped at 11.45. Under Michael Barton Surrey gained their first honour since 1914, when in 1950 we shared the title with Lancashire. The progress was halted in 1951 and the County slipped back to sixth position. Calls of business saw the resignation of Michael Barton, who could look back with satisfaction on his three years in office, and the appointment of Stuart Surridge, who had played a full season in 1951, as Surrey's new captain was announced.

The years that followed became unique in the history of the County Championship. Stuart Surridge led Surrey to five consecutive Championships before retiring and handing over to Peter May, who in 1957 and 1958 carried on the good work.

The detailed results are as follows:

	Played	Won	Lost	Drawn	No decision	Points	Title Won by
1952	28	20	3	5	0	256	32 pts
1953	28	13	4	10	1	184	16 pts
1954	28	15	3	8	2	208	22 pts
1955	28	23	5	0	0	284	16 pts
1956	28	15	5	6	2	200	20 pts
1957	28	21	3	3	1	312	94 pts
1958	28	14	5	8	1	212	26 pts

During that period no fewer than seven of us were frequently absent on Test duty. Peter May, Alec Bedser, Tony Lock, Peter Loader, Arthur McIntyre, Ken Barrington and myself totalled no less than 149 Test match appearances. This underlines the fact that insufficient praise was given to an army of talented reserves, many of whom could have furthered their careers with other counties. Numbered amongst them were Dennis Cox, Alan Brazier, the brothers Pratt, John McMahon, Geoff Kirby, Raman Subba Row, Mike Willett, David Gibson and many others.

The format of this fine side varied only slightly over the full seven years and eight of the side, namely the Bedsers, Fletcher, Constable, Clark, McIntyre, Lock and myself saw it through from start to finish. Fishlock, Parker, Whittaker and Surridge himself had departed in succession, and over that period of time were replaced by May, Loader, Barrington and Stewart, all Test match cricketers.

The two Peters, May and Loader, became regulars in 1953 and I have always believed that their arrival added the finishing touches to a side which had promised much but fell that fraction short of being championship leaders. Peter May gave us the extra runs we needed and Peter Loader, the finest new ball bowler I have ever seen, completed our varied quartet with the ball.

Fate had decided that four Test match bowlers should reach their peak at the same time and all play together in the same side. Alec Bedser, Tony Lock, Peter Loader and myself totalled 642 Test match wickets alone and one cannot imagine this sort of situation existing in any County side before or since.

Big Alec, in simplest terms, was the greatest medium-fast bowler I have ever seen and am ever likely to see. His massive frame, wonderfully co-ordinated in an easy 12-yard run up, produced the copy book action for a bowler of his type. Little wonder that I cannot recall any damaged muscles – quite remarkable when you consider that his career spanned over 20 years, and often included 1,000 overs per year. His stock delivery was the inswinger, and his

Celebrating another championship, after May, Loader, Barrington and Stewart had strengthened the side. *From left:* Eric Bedser, Stuart Surridge, Peter May, Arthur McIntyre, myself, Peter Loader, Alec Bedser, Tony Lock, Ken Barrington, Mickey Stewart, Bernard Constable.

control was such that he could make the ball swing in at the last possible second. He never concerned himself with the outswinger. Instead he quietly developed the leg cutter to such an extent that on any pitch on which the ball would grip he was virtually unplayable.

Wiry and slightly-built Loader could make a new ball talk. He had the uncanny knack of bowling an outswinger from both close to the stumps and also from the very end of the return crease and he could do the same thing with the inswinger. No quick bowler of his era could better his change of pace, and he could often bowl successively a slow off spinner and the most vicious of bouncers. Many doubted the legality of these two deliveries and observing them so often from close quarters I could not disagree.

For several years also there was a grave doubt about the legality of a fair percentage of Tony Lock's deliveries, brought about by his sudden change from a slow flighty non-spinner to a vicious tweaker of the ball at near medium pace. I must say there was lot of justification for it.

Fair or unfair, Tony was a tremendous competitor. He gave everything he had at all times, so often bowling his 30 overs in acute pain when lesser mortals would have had their feet up in the dressing room. Working as a combination brought the best out of both of us and even now, though 12,000 miles and not 22 yards separate us, we still keep well in touch and remain the firmest of friends.

With any match-winning combination in any sport there are always the knockers, those who look to undermine success. The principal accusations thrown at Surrey were first the factor that the pitch was especially prepared for the spinners Lock and myself and second that the team spirit was not what it should be. Discounting rain-affected wickets I can recall a mere half a dozen ill-prepared pitches during the entire seven years, and whilst critics will remember these they conveniently forget an equal number of pitches which gave the finest bowlers no hope whatsoever. Middlesex had no cause for complaint in scoring 537 for 2 and on two occasions the West Indies total exceeded 500. Northants scored 529 for 9 in reply to Surrey's 378 for 5 and totals over 350 are too numerous to mention. I was omitted from two Australian tours for being labelled an Oval bowler, yet of the 1,944 wickets in my career only 680 at 17 apiece were taken on the ground where I played far more than one third of my cricket. My overall career record at Lords was slightly superior to that at the Oval, while visits to the Gloucester grounds brought me 56 wickets at a mere 10 runs apiece. Overseas, on the rock hard pitches where I had previously been politely told by selectors that off spin was a waste of time, my bowling averages were as follows:

Adelaide	10	Johannesburg	17	Bombay	18
Brisbane	11	Cape Town	17	Georgetown	22
Sydney	15	Durban	17	Barbados	23

One hopes therefore that the myth of the Oval wickets is finally laid to rest.

The people who complained about the behaviour of the side on the field would certainly take it all back if they spent much time watching present day antics. Could anyone imagine Alec Bedser embracing Arthur McIntyre for a leg side stumping, or the entire side engulfing Stuart Surridge after a slip catch safely held? Of course there were niggles when things were going wrong but this is something which was not unique to Surrey or cricket in general and can be found in every walk of life.

Those of us who had been fortunate enough to play for England had an enormous respect for Fletcher, Constable, Clark and Eric Bedser and knew that we could never have achieved such a remarkable run without them. Certain and positive proof of the great spirit, comradeship and friendliness engendered in that side of

16

The championship side of the 1950s forms of a large part of the Surrey County Cricket Golfers Association of the 1970s. Twenty years on we still play our shots, this one of mine being at Stoke Poges Golf Club in 1977.

the 1950s can still be seen 20 years later. With the exception of our two Australian emigrants, Lock and Loader, the side of the 1950s forms the very heart of the Surrey County Cricket Golfers Association. We play a dozen games a year, and if the percentage of successes against the Golf Clubs which kindly act as our hosts does not match our cricket performances, there remains as there always will the very essence of team spirit and goodwill, unrivalled wherever the game has been played.

Perhaps I may be excused in singling out one of the members of this all conquering team on the grounds of my own involvement. Prior to my arrival at Kennington Oval it seemed fairly certain that Eric Bedser was destined to become Surrey's principal off spinner for a good number of years. Instead he was forced to take a back seat and on very many occasions was used only as a fourth change bowler. On helpful pitches he held only a watching brief, and on good wickets one can easily imagine what went through his mind when he was tossed the ball after there had been no joy for Bedser (A), Loader, Lock or Laker. With an enormous pair of hands he could spin the ball like a top and with any other County he must have topped 100 wickets per season. Bearing these facts in mind, his career total of 833 wickets at 25 runs each, added to his 15,000 runs and a top score of 163, made him a most valued all-rounder. Those figures, in fact, are very similar to the career figures of Tony Greig at the time of writing. There were many who ridiculed the Bedser Boys as twins and believed that they overplayed the identical twin situation as a publicity stunt. Those of us close to them over so many years know nothing was further from the truth. They were and remain to this day totally devoted to each other.

Over the years I have never wavered in my opinion that Stuart Surridge was the finest captain under whom I ever played. As I mentioned previously his appointment was by no means welcomed by all at the Oval, where the vast majority of Surrey captains had arrived via Oxford or Cambridge. Stuart was an Old Emmanuel from Wandsworth who had played a fair amount of Surrey second eleven cricket, and his chief qualification in those days seemed to be the fact that he was a member of the unpaid ranks. The professional staff certainly did not expect him to be any better or worse than his predecessors but at least we knew him as a sincere and friendly colleague, a genuine amateur who would try to give all of us a fair crack of the whip.

Possibly we did not appreciate immediately how much he respected the ability of the individuals he had inherited. As this became quickly apparent to us our respect for Stuart as a leader and a competitor grew in leaps and bounds. There were those who were somewhat cynical of him as a cricketer, a view I could never share. On occasions he bowled really well. It is worth noting that in a

relatively short first-class career he took no less than 506 wickets, which included 7 for 49 against a strong Lancashire side. Equipped, understandably, with the best piece of willow in the business (he makes bats) he cracked many useful runs in the lower order. Probably his unhappiest day was to fall 13 runs short of a maiden century against Wilf Wooller's Glamorgan.

It was as a close catcher that he will probably be best remembered. Utterly fearless, he oozed confidence and firmly believed he could catch anything close to the wicket. He wanted and indeed expected a catch from every ball that came down. So often the good slip fielder, after dropping a couple of catches, hopes and prays that another will not quickly come his way. Not so Stuart Surridge. After a miss he desperately needed another chance to show the batsman how fortunate he had been. There is no doubt that this attitude of mind inspired Messrs Lock, Stewart and

One of Stuart Surridge's greatest qualities as a captain was the example he set as a magnificent short leg fieldsman. Here he catches Vigar of Essex off my bowling at the Oval.

20

Barrington, and thanks to the skipper Surrey produced a magnificent quartet of close fieldsmen.

These alone were not the only qualities of a captain whose record surpasses anything before or since. He had the happy knack of bringing the best out of each individual player and was shrewd enough to appreciate that he could not handle, for instance, Tony Lock in the same manner as Alec Bedser. His approach to Peter Loader varied considerably from his attitude towards me.

I certainly have Stuart to thank on the occasion of my all 10 Australian wickets for Surrey in 1956. Feeling far from 100 per cent fit when I arrived at the Oval that morning due to a very rough night with two sick children, I was hoping that we would bat first on a pretty good wicket. It was not to be, and shortly I was in the middle of a long yet most productive spell. An unbroken session of 30 overs had brought me the first six Australian wickets, by which

Left: Not the Surridge style, but I'm glad to say I held George Dawkes of Derbyshire off Alec Bedser at the Oval, 1956.

Right: The Australian second innings at the Oval in 1956, when Surrey became the first County team to beat them since 1912. For a change this batsman, Len Maddocks, is c Laker b Lock. Note Tony's attacking field. The other fielders are Barrington, Surridge, Swetman (wicket-keeper), Fletcher, Cox and May. 'Slasher' Mackay is the other Aussie batsman.

time I suggested to Stuart that I was just about on my knees and we had sufficiently good bowlers to polish off the remaining Australians. He would have none of it, and over the next hour and a half he cajoled and persuaded me to keep having another couple of overs. Finally after 46 overs I had all 10 wickets to my name and the most delighted person at the Oval was the Surrey captain.

He won very many famous victories for us, none more so than when we beat Worcestershire by an innings, after he had shocked the crowd and stunned his own team into silence when declaring at 92 for 3 with a first innings lead of 67. Whatever the situation he always looked for a positive result. Winning meant everything to him and he frequently reminded all and sundry that 'you get nothing for coming second'. Consequently he has always looked back with particular pride to 1955, when of the 28 County championship matches, 23 were won, 5 lost and not a single game drawn. Yorkshire, who had a wonderful side that year, finished runners-up and they, like us, broke the record for the number of points scored in a season. Only 16 points separated the two of us.

Not a single representative honour came Stuart's way, for incredibly there remained at Lords a hard core who never regarded him as a cricketer or a captain. There is no doubt that he should have skippered the Gentlemen, particularly when one considers some of the ragbag cricketers selected; and what a good choice he would have made for a minor overseas tour. He certainly did not lose any sleep over it, for he was very much a man of Surrey, where

his real love truly lay, and where his achievements are unparalleled.

By the end of 1958 the pressure of maintaining consecutive championship wins had become too much and there were minor cracks appearing in Surrey's match-winning combination. Fishlock and Parker had long since gone and Whitaker had moved on to Jersey. The Bedser brothers and Arthur McIntyre were past 40 and Bernard Constable was 38. Tom Clark was waging a gallant battle against the dreaded arthritis of the hip, Peter Loader had one eye on Australia as his home of the future and the call of business meant Peter May's days as a Surrey cricketer were also numbered. I knew that because of an arthritic condition of my spinning finger, which at times I could scarcely bend, 1959 would be my last serious season.

No one could possibly begrudge Yorkshire their success in ending our long run, though it took them to 1 September before we were finally relegated to a joint runners-up position.

After the years of plenty it was fairly certain that there would be lean times to follow, but sadly there has been little for the faithful Ovalites to rejoice about over the past 20 years. A scrambling Championship success in 1971 has been the solitary solace in the three-day game, scant reward when one considers the talented players who have come and gone during that time. Mickey Stewart captained the side skilfully, unselfishly and with a good deal of courage. Alongside him Ken Barrington and John Edrich were just about the two best English batsmen of their era. Geoff Arnold, when in the right frame of mind, was the most dangerous opening bowler

in the country. At 19 Pat Pocock looked like being a world beater and much the same could have been said of Younis when he first appeared at the age of 17. Intikhab was good enough to exceed 100 Test wickets.

Having been banished into the cricket wilderness for seven years after publishing *Over to Me* (Muller, 1960) I was consequently not in a position to evaluate the problems that had arisen. Initially the players had a good deal of my sympathy, for it seemed that they were forever being reminded about and compared to the sides of the 1950s, which was totally unfair. I sensed that this was still the case when I ended my term of exile and spent some time in the players' dressing room. Therefore I purposely refrained from talking about bygone days unless I was asked a specific question. Players began to search for plausible excuses to account for their lack of success instead of rolling up their sleeves and trying that little bit harder. They could, in fact, have done with an injection of six Robin Jackmans!

Some remarkable decisions also emanated from the Committee Room, none more so than the one which saw Bob Willis fit to tour with England but not good enough for a Surrey cap. His departure for Warwickshire followed by Selvey's to Middlesex and Roger Knight's to Gloucestershire proved to be serious errors of judgement. In a little over ten years Saturday gates had fallen from

Most of the men who made Surrey great in the 1950s. The players are, *left to right, back:* Ron Pratt, Derek Pratt, Peter Loader, Tom Clark, Ken Barrington, Dennis Cox, Mickey Stewart. *Front:* Alan Brazier, myself, Eric Bedser, Peter May, Stuart Surridge, Alec Bedser, Arthur McIntyre, Tony Lock, Bernard Constable, David Fletcher and Roy Swetman. In civvies are two old Surrey stalwarts, Herbert Strudwick, *left,* and Andy Sandham, *right.*

24

15,000 to a mere trickle, the County was slipping further into the red and the professional staff had been reduced to a mere 14 or 15 players. There was no money to buy an overseas player at the time that Sobers, Lloyd, Richards and Procter made their bows. In common with most other counties, Surrey had kept their members' subscriptions rate at a ridiculously low figure, thus losing thousands of pounds of vital revenue. The grandiose schemes for major development of the Oval met with every conceivable obstruction.

That Surrey survived just about the stickiest financial period in their history was principally due to three factors. One-day cricket brought not only better gates but a share-out of sponsors' money, Test matches continued to draw fine crowds and the recently formed Promotion, Public Relations and Publicity Committee proved to be a wonderful innovation. This last was largely due to the untiring efforts of Bernie Coleman and Raman Subba Row. The former, a cricket fanatic and most loyal supporter since schooldays, believed the time had come to sell the game of cricket both commercially and to the public in general. His keen and alert business acumen and his determination to see Surrey cricket succeed was a prime factor in the financial recovery of the County. Raman's thinking was along similar lines and his total commitment to the task in hand left him with precious little leisure time or spare hours.

For a couple of years I was a member of this committee and had first hand experience of the great work accomplished by those two devotees. I felt very strongly however, that any assistance I could offer should be concerned with cricket rather than promotion, but despite several attempts by various committee colleagues to channel my efforts in this direction, the door to the cricket committee was firmly shut in my face. There were those who still remembered *Over to Me*, and others who rejected me because I employed a business agent. It was all extremely hard to understand, particularly as Surrey cricket was at such a low ebb and I had forgotten more about the game than some of the committee members would ever know. To further confuse matters I suddenly found myself, along with Peter May and Ken Barrington, made an Honorary Life Member of Surrey CCC. This is an honour which falls to only a privileged few and in some ways meant more to me than anything I had previously achieved in my cricketing life.

Then quite suddenly a few years later, early in 1978 to be precise, Alfred Gover, now installed as Chairman of Cricket, invited me to go forward as a nominee for a place on the cricket committee. Rightly or wrongly I rejected this offer for two reasons. Firstly I failed to see why I should enter into a ballot, and secondly the cricket committee had grown to such gigantic proportions as to make me just another voice. Perhaps the increase in numbers was an

effort to ensure that at last there would a reasonable number of committee members in attendance during play at the Oval. Whether or not this proved to be the case I do not know, but apparently it did lead to abormally long meetings and more frustration. For a long time I have been an advocate of small select committees believing that no more than six knowledgeable members closely in touch with Surrey cricket was an absolute maximum.

The 1978 season proved to be disastrous for Surrey. In the County Championship they were spared the ignominy of being wooden spoonists by a cat's whisker, they made little progress in Cup competitions and finished in the lower reaches of the John Player League. For the first time ever the Club was faced with a minor members revolt and feeling ran high in the Long Room. As this unhappy season was coming to an end, club Chairman Raman Subba Row contacted me, principally to see if I had any thoughts on how Surrey cricket might be improved. His assessment of what should be done and my own were just about identical, and consequently he asked me if I would form a small working party consisting of the two of us together with Ken Barrington and Micky Stewart to see if we could reach a successful format for the improvement of Surrey cricket.

I felt sure we could make progress. To begin with, the performance of many of the players did not reflect their ability, and to remedy this I believed the most important step was to appoint a cricket manager. A person to act in a similar capacity to that of a soccer manager was vital. At the time of writing this suggestion is under discussion and I trust an appointment is imminent, but already a spearhead pace bowler has been recruited and several feelers have been put out in regard to a general strengthening of the playing staff. As I see it Surrey have the base of three or four first-class batsmen, a top-class spinner, an excellent medium-fast bowler and a wicket-keeper full of promise. Provided one or two of the youngsters make normal progress and more spirit is injected into the team as a whole, there is positively no reason why some real improvement should not be forthcoming.

An association of 32 years with one Club is a vast chunk out of anyone's life and is bound to contain pleasant and lasting memories in addition to days of worry and drama. There is no doubt that with me the former heavily outweigh the latter. Without ever wishing to disown my birth place, Kennington Oval remains very special to me. To this day I have never taken it for granted, and even now retain the sense of hope, excitement and anticipation whenever I drive through the Hobbs Gate that I experienced the first time.

Old Trafford

In my early days no self-respecting Yorkshire lad could look in any way kindly at Lancashire County Cricket Club. By the age of 16 I had crossed the Pennines only once, and that for a one-day choir trip to Grange over Sands.

Whenever the visiting marauders came over in full cry we boys were early into the ground at Park Avenue, Bradford before the Lancashire trains unloaded at the Exchange Station. The rivalry was so intense as to be almost unbelievable. A victory was worth 10 weeks pocket money, and on the rare occasions when the visitors went off with the points there was utter despair on the Shipley bus. I hated every single that Eddie Paynter scored and despised the shrieking antics of George Duckworth behind the stumps. Years later we were to become the staunchest of friends!

The war, I suppose, melted my partisan outlook, for there were many changes in those six long years. The great Yorkshire side of the 1930s simply disintegrated. Hedley Verity was gone and never to return. Sutcliffe, Mitchell, Barber and Wood retired, and Sellers, Bowes, Smailes and Turner struggled on only for a couple of seasons, and were mere shadows of their former selves. Only Hutton,

Above: My old friend John Ikin, one of the best-ever close fielders, catches Eric Rowan of South Africa off my bowling in the 1951 Test at Old Trafford. Godfrey Evans is the wicket-keeper and Len Hutton the other short leg. *Preceding page:* Old Trafford, a ground with great memories for me, and where there is always a new friend to remind me of 1956.

30

The England team at Old Trafford in 1951 with autographs. *Left to right, back:* Willie Watson, Tom Graveney, Roy Tattersall, myself, Brian Statham, John Ikin. *Front:* Alec Bedser, Reg Simpson, Freddie Brown, Len Hutton, Godfrey Evans. Plenty of slow bowlers, including two off-spinners!

Yardley and Robinson were left to carry the flag. The replacements included several players I had played with and against in League cricket and however much one appreciated the obvious talents of Wilson, Watson, Wardle and company one could not look upon them with the same awe and wonderment reserved for the heroes of boyhood. Coincidental with all this was the fact that I had begun to appreciate that Lancashire players were also human beings. In fact, the Lancashire side I first encountered was as great a bunch of fellows as you could wish to meet.

My subsequent association with Lancashire was based on a long and lasting friendship with John Ikin and if there is a more respected cricketer who ever laced up a pair of boots, I have yet to meet him. Winston Place, Roy Tattersall, Brian Statham and Ken Grieves all fall into the same category, and almost before I was aware of it I no longer gave a tinker's cuss on the outcome of a Roses battle.

Due simply to the fact that I was lucky enough to take 19 wickets in a single game at Manchester (and you need more than your fair share of good fortune to do that) my name will forever be associated with Old Trafford. The events of this historic contest have been

31

recorded often enough to excuse my going into detail, but oddly enough one or two aspects of it have never been mentioned.

Many people mistakenly believed that Old Trafford was a happy hunting ground for me but prior to 1956 my record there was abysmal, judged on my own standards. My first ever visit took place in 1948 when I was 26, selected in the twelve for the Australian Test. I was not surprised to be relegated to twelfth man. The following year I appeared again, this time against New Zealand, when I was omitted once more to allow the 18-year-old Brian Close to make his Test match debut. This time I accepted my omission with a good deal less equanimity. There was no method by which I could consider Brian a better off spinner than myself, and in those days he was delegated to bat at number nine. Jealousy exists as much in cricket as in any other walk of life and I can never seriously believe that one can be expected to wish that the man who takes your job will be a big success. There was no dream debut for young Close, whose one wicket cost 85 runs and came via a full toss which was caught at deep square leg. He also failed to score with the bat, falling to a boundary catch.

Still I had no cause either for celebration when in 1950 I made my first ever appearance at Old Trafford against the West Indians. Having taken 8 wickets for 2 runs in the Test Trial, I simply had to play but I bowled abominably, returning home thoroughly dejected with figures of 1 for 86. Four wickets against the South Africans in 1951 was an improvement, but Manchester in 1952 against India belonged to Fred Trueman and Tony Lock and I bowled but two overs in the match. Prior to 1956 my last Test appearance was against Hassett's Australians when my three wickets cost 53.

Thus I had travelled north on six occasions to Manchester, played in four Tests and collected a paltry eight wickets at a cost of 235. Hardly the figures to fill a bowler with confidence. During this period of ten years I played precious little cricket against Lancashire, only appearing at Old Trafford on three occasions for a total of 11 for 242. In all then, seven first-class games had produced 19 wickets at 25 apiece. Little wonder that thoughts of a world record performance never entered my head at Manchester in 1956.

A second piece of statistical evidence about the game emerged fairly recently thanks to the industry of Irving Rosenwater. It transpired that the entire Australian side that played at Manchester was composed of first-class centurions, nine of them with Test match hundreds to their name. Furthermore Irving discovered that each and every one of my 46 victims in that Test series could be credited with a century in first-class cricket. Of our 16 English cricketers who toured Pakistan and New Zealand in 1977/78 only seven had reached three figures in first-class cricket and only two

The young Brian Close in 1949, when to my disgust he was preferred as the off-spinner in the England side at Old Trafford to play New Zealand.

32

Brian Statham, the last Test match bowler of real international class produced by Lancashire.

had made a Test match hundred. Have batting standards really fallen away to such an extent?

I was by no means the only cricketer who, playing for his county at Old Trafford, has been strongly advised upon going out to bat not to close the gate as he shall be on his way back before long. Yet the reception accorded me by the self-same members on Test match days used to leave me wondering if I had been born and bred in Wigan. At least I knew exactly where I stood with the Lancashire crowd and the passing of the years has not changed them. Since my playing days I have spent more time at Lancashire headquarters than I ever did as a player. The ground and the crowd have grown familiar to me and I find it almost impossible to walk ten yards without being stopped for a chat and I enjoy every minute of it.

'I were there, tha knows, and it were a great day" is reckoned to be sufficient to recall 1956. Mind you it is also quite likely to be 'Nay, lad, tha were wrong what tha said about Frank 'Ayes' or 'And what dost tha think about Clive Lloyd now?"

Sadly these diehard supporters have had little to enthuse about and but for the advent of limited over cricket Lancashire must have been hard pushed to survive. They did so thanks initially to winning the John Player League title during the first two years of the

competition and following this up by taking a firm grip on the
Gillette Cup, carrying the trophy away from Lords four times in the
space of six years. Enthusiastic crowds filled Old Trafford to
bursting point on so many memorable occasions and the massive
gate receipts helped to subsidise county cricket when, in dire
contrast, the attendance was, to say the least, pathetic.

Quite incredibly, apart from a half share in the 1950 County
Championship, it is 45 years since Lancashire took the title. How is
it then that a side with a striking success rate in one-day cricket has
failed totally to be in contention for the County Championships?
Could it be that the county have failed to produce a single bowler of
real international standard since Brian Statham first appeared close
on 30 years ago? I say this with due deference to Peter Lever and
Ken Higgs. Attractive batting and accurate bowling is a sound
recipe for one day cricket. Lancashires' successes were built on that
type of foundation. Engineer and the brilliant Clive Lloyd led many
a run chase backed by the fine performances of David Lloyd, Barry
Wood and Frank Hayes. Visiting batsmen were kept in check by
Lever and Lee plus the accurate spin of Hughes and Simmons and,
by no means least, the nagging medium pace of Barry Wood. The
last-named with a cupboard full of gold awards has produced his
overs at the minimum cost.

However to win matches over three days one must bowl out the
opposition twice and to do this you need match-winning bowlers. At
the time of writing Wood has taken five wickets in a first-class match
on only seven occasions, Simmons on 13, Hughes on 18 and Lee on

23. Compare these figures with those of Statham and Trueman, who each did it over 100 times, a figure also surpassed by both Illingworth and Underwood, whilst Fred Titmus achieved the feat no fewer than 168 times. Thus Lancashire have badly missed bowlers of this category.

Full credit should be paid to the Lancashire Committee for looking after their players, for throughout these years the Committee have seen to it that their professional staff have been the highest paid in the country. When the Packer saga first hit the headlines and the pay of the average county cricketer came under close scrutiny and censure, the chairman of Lancashire CCC told me that for the five months that their players were employed during the summer they could expect to earn something between £700 – £800 per month in basic salaries. There must, however, be some searching questions to be asked of them in relation to the acute shortage of top-class cricketers emerging from the County and in particular about the quality of the coaching standards. In pre-war years players like the Tyldesleys, Duckworth, Washbrook and Paynter came off the assembly lines of the various leagues and it is hard to believe that sources of so much talent have dried up. I recall making a note of Andrew Kennedy and John Abrahams during their early games but to date their progress has slowed.

The classic example of coaching failure must surely be Frank Hayes. Now here was a young man with a great deal of natural ability who looked every inch an England batsman in the making and who, I believe, should have become a fixture in our national side. Although there were a few chinks in his technique there seemed no reason why they should not be ironed out, but five years later it seemed that he was still making the same errors – which left me, for one, in some doubt as to whether the faults had been spotted or whether, if they had, any effort had been made to put them right. Perhaps a leaf could have been taken out of Geoffrey Boycott's book. Sobers had caused him a few problems during a West Indies tour and after being dismissed by Sobers at Leeds, Boycott spent a good hour in our BBC wagon watching the replay time after time until he was positive he had worked out a solution. So many modern aids like this are now available to our cricketers and, of course, to our coaches.

Having spoken to clubs and societies throughout Lancashire and witnessed a netfull of 11-year-olds working hard in midwinter at the fine East Lancashire CC, I am in no doubt that latent talent still abounds in the county of the Red Rose. My own strong attachment to Old Trafford makes me look forward to the day when another Paynter, Washbrook, Statham or Tattersall appears out of the very heart of Lancashire and makes the Red Rose once again a real force in the land.

Trent Bridge

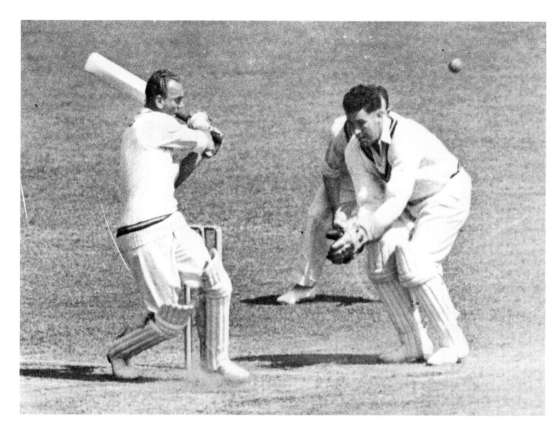

The Oval and Lord's apart, I have spent more time playing cricket at Trent Bridge than at any other ground in the world. Nowhere have I discovered a more pleasant atmosphere, better comradeship or a more sporting crowd. It matters not whether you are a player, an official, a member of the Press, Radio, Television or just a spectator, there is a feeling of being made welcome the instant one enters the gate.

In my playing days the Nottinghamshire v Surrey fixture was the traditional Bank Holiday game, and I cannot ever recall missing our annual Whitsuntide visit to Nottingham. Invariably blessed with glorious weather and with 25,000 people packed inside, those days remain memories to cherish. The opposition were truly men of Nottinghamshire. Keeton, Harris, Hardstaff, Simpson, Butler, Jepson and Woodhead formed the basis of a side many of whom remain firm friends, and they still retain their Trent Bridge connections. There was a rapport between our two teams second to none. Fierce and intense rivalry throughout the long hot days was followed always by a few draughts of cooling beverage together in the Trent Bridge Inn and a chat about the events of the day.

My old friend Joe Hardstaff was a regular on these occasions. Son of a famous father (Joe Senior), his own offspring (Joe Junior,

Above: Joe Hardstaff, an old friend at Notts, hooking against Middlesex in 1949. Leslie Compton is the wicket-keeper.
Previous page: The ground at Trent Bridge, where I spent many a Whitsun holiday period playing for Surrey and many an evening discussing the cricket with the men of Notts.

Above: Gary Sobers, the best all-rounder the game has seen, but not able to produce his best week in and week out for Notts.

Junior), who was just about into his teens, would wait patiently by the front door. Several years later I went down to Eastbourne to play for a Robins XI v the RAF and was greeted by a giant of a man, whose massive frame blocked the entrance to the pavilion doors. 'Hello, Jim, how nice to see you, come and meet the RAF boys'. He observed my puzzled expression. 'Surely you remember me?'' That remark was of no help. 'I used to wait for you all outside the TBI whilst father and you were enjoying yourselves''. Of course, it was young Joe. Then came a small whisper 'You will give me one off the mark for the sake of old Dad?' We fielded first and while I was bowling out strode Joe at number four. He carefully took guard with a bat which seemed no more than a size five in his hand, yet which I subsequently discovered weighed 2 lb 10 oz. I gave him a nod and tossed up a slow inviting half volley. Joe let fly. As it screamed past my left hand I made a gesture of an attempted caught and bowled, but no more than a gesture. I followed the flight quickly enough to note mid-off taking evasive action. The only action the fielder in front of the sightscreen took was to gaze in bewilderment as the ball continued its upward flight, and for all we knew it may well have disturbed the deck chair inhabitants on the sea front. 'One off the mark' turned out to be the biggest six I have ever seen.

Young Joe had ambitions to play for Nottinghamshire but Dad would have none of it. His judgement was correct. Joe still idolises his father but he has remained eternally grateful to him for encouraging him to make his life in the RAF where he has had a most distinguished career.

Trent Bridge has a reputation for good batting pitches and this standard has been maintained with a greater degree of consistency than any other ground I know. Since the hard, true, fast, marled pitches of the Larwood and Voce era there has been a succession of top class groundsmen and one can never recall the whole playing area looking anything but a picture. It was for many years a bowler's graveyard and my heart bled for Harold Butler, Arthur Jepson and Frank Woodhead who toiled away day in and day out on a wicket which reduced the bowlers to mediocrity and gave ordinary batsmen an inflated sense of their abilities. It speaks volumes for their character that they managed to keep a sense of humour.

In 1947 Notts made 401 on the Saturday and by Monday evening we had passed their score. Resuming on Tuesday morning both Jack Parker and Errol Holmes made hundreds before lunch when we declared at 706 for 4. Needless to say the match was drawn, but 1,308 runs were scored in the three days for the loss of 18 wickets. Two years later a total of 1,018 runs were scored with only 19 wickets going down and in 1955 1,111 were made in a match. Walter Keeton, who played Alec Bedser better than anyone in the game, Joe Hardstaff and Reg Simpson revelled in the run riots and of course there was always Charlie Harris. If there was a greater character then I never met him. Completely unpredictable, a law unto himself, the cricket stories that surround him are unending. He infuriated Freddie Brown with a running commentary on every ball he faced. As soon as the ball left Freddie's hand he would shout down the wicket 'It's a leg break' or 'It's a googly'. I recall facing Harold Butler one day with the new ball in front of 20,000 spectators with Charlie half a dozen yards away in the gully. Suddenly Harold, in full flight, was rudely interrupted by a great shout from Charlie. Having stopped the bowler he then addressed his remarks to me 'I feel its only fair to tell you that unbeknown to you we've got a second gully'. I glanced a couple of yards away to his right and

Clive Rice, a pleasant surprise for Notts, as he became an outstanding cricketer only after Notts had brought him from South Africa.

40

there glistening in the sunshine lay Charlie's complete top and bottom set of false teeth. Sadly he was stricken with cancer yet when Alec Bedser and I visited him in hospital he was still full of his inimitable humour. After a partial recovery, the dreaded disease caught up with him again and he died at the age of 45. Unhappily they do not come like Charlie any more.

In more recent times three superb all-round cricketers, all from overseas, Bruce Dooland, Gary Sobers and Clive Rice, have graced Trent Bridge. No one could possibly argue that Sobers has proved himself the most brilliant all-rounder the game has seen, but from Nottinghamshire's viewpoint Dooland made the greatest contribution to the County. If there was a suspicion that the wicket was eased sufficiently to accommodate his bowling, his performances were unparalleled. Doubtless if he had remained in Australia he would have become an automatic Test match choice but instead he came to England to play League cricket, where he met with enormous success. To prove his potential he played for Notts for five seasons before returning home and in that time he captured no less than 808 wickets and scored 5,175 runs.

The signing of Gary Sobers at a then unheard-of salary for a professional cricketer seemed an inspired decision. He was 32 years of age and played for a further seven years. To all intents and purposes he should have been at the peak of his career but he had already played cricket at the highest level, summer and winter, for 14 years without sparing himself and the strain was beginning to tell. Of course there were magical moments yet it remained a strange fact that in the County Championship he never did himself full justice. Towards the end of his sixth season he looked tired and weary and appeared to have lost his appetite for a form of cricket which is so demanding.

If Nottinghamshire lost out on the Sobers gamble then they must have been pleasantly surprised with the subsequent performances of Clive Rice. This South African, hardly rated in his own country, has proved himself to be an outstanding cricketer. His aggressive fluent stroke play and his lively medium-paced bowling have endeared him to the faithful Nottinghamshire supporters. His fine 1978 season saw him quite rightly rewarded as the Bonusbond cricketer of the year.

As a Test match innings Stan McCabe's memorable 232 at Trent Bridge in 1938 will live for ever. This was the day when Don Bradman exhorted his team not to miss a ball of it as they would never see the like of such batting again.

Ten years later I played my first Test match against Bradman's all-conquering Australians. Even so our batting line up of Hutton, Washbrook, Edrich, Compton, Hardstaff and Barnett looked equally formidable. We were happy to win the toss and for half an hour it seemed that Len and Cyril were on their way to another fine opening partnership when heavy rain suspended play. How the story changed when play was resumed. On a now damp wicket, Lindwall, Miller and Johnston tore us apart and I suddenly found myself going in to bat for an over before tea with the English score 74 for 7. As Norman Yardley and I emerged to face the music after the break I recall him saying 'You know what two Yorkshiremen do when they find themselves in this sort of situation – they get stuck in and battle their way out of it'. Poor Norman fell to Ernie Toshack the very first ball after tea and we were 74 for 8. However the wicket had eased considerably and Lindwall was out of the attack with a strained muscle. Alec Bedser and I shared a partnership of 89 and my 63 remained my highest score in Test cricket.

Bedser, Edrich, Barnett and Young all had a bowl before I came on. I quickly bowled Arthur Morris for 31, had Sid Barnes brilliantly caught by Godfrey Evans and to my great delight trapped Keith Miller for a duck, to have the first three wickets for a personal cost of 22. Bill Brown, normally an opener, joined Don Bradman and much to my chagrin Norman Yardley took the new ball. When I came back for a second spell Bradman was nearing another hundred and Hassett was equally well set. For all that I had a high regard for Norman Yardley as a captain. He had a deep knowledge of the game as he has since demonstrated with his radio and television summaries. I have always been surprised that he has not been used more often.

In 1957 I spent the hardest and toughest five days of my whole career on the lovely Trent Bridge ground when we played the third Test match against the West Indies. The game was played during a heat wave on the easiest of Trent Bridge wickets and for some unaccountable reason the selectors omitted Tony Lock and we were sent out with only four front-line bowlers. To make matters worse Trevor Bailey ricked his back and had to be sparingly used. West Indies used eight bowlers to no avail as we reached a mammoth first innings total of 619 for 6 thanks to Tom Graveney (258), Peter Richardson (126) and Peter May (104). The declaration came during the tea interval on the second day. West Indies first innings of 372 was dominated by a masterly undefeated 191 by Frank Worrell who carried his bat. It had taken us 151 overs to dismiss the opposition with our depleted attack and with the temperature still in the eighties.

Pressing for victory, Peter May decided to enforce the follow on and at one stage we had West Indies at 89 for 5 with Worrell, Sobers, Walcott, Kanhai and Weekes all back in the pavilion. It was then that the late and lamented Collie Smith played a most remarkable innings. Many pundits believe that if you played Statham off the back foot you were as good as dead. Collie on this

The England team at Trent Bridge in 1956 – alas, no Notts players. *Left to right, back:* Jim Parks, Peter Richardson, Colin Cowdrey, Alan Moss, Bob Appleyard, Tom Graveney, Tony Lock. *Front:* Willie Watson, Trevor Bailey, Peter May, myself, Godfrey Evans.

day hit the great Lancashire fast bowler off his back foot straight into the pavilion. He was safely past three figures when the second new ball was due. Even the great strength of Fred Trueman had begun to wane and as he came back with his loosener prior to taking the new ball he was greeted by our spectators thus 'Trueman – you're no quicker than bloody Laker'. This brought a glare and a curse from Fred who directed himself to Collie Smith. He bowled him three perfect outswingers and the batsman played and missed all three. Fred straddled himself in the middle of the pitch, arms akimbo, giving himself a few seconds to recover his breath 'Smith' he said, 'going to bloody Ireland tomorrow, are you? Tha's no need for thee to fly, tha can bloody walk there'. For all that it was a great performance by Collie who went on to 168, and West Indies lasted until 5 o'clock on the final afternoon and a draw was inevitable.

We had, therefore, been in the field in the unrelenting heat from 4.30 on Friday until 5 o'clock on Tuesday. Statham had bowled 70 overs, Trueman 55 and my own contribution was 105 overs. I had lost 7 lb in weight and been paid considerably less than £1 per over. Interesting to note that off spinner Geoff Miller's payment in last

43

The exciting Trent Bridge Test of 1977. Rodney Marsh out lbw to debutant Ian Botham, who took five Australian wickets in his first Test innings as a bowler.

year's Trent Bridge test was roughly £200 per over. It is good that times have changed for the better. At the time it was most gratifying for me to receive, in company with Fred and Brian, a charming letter from 'Gubby' Allen, chairman of the selectors, thanking us for our effort.

Let me establish once again that I do not harbour one scrap of jealousy of any modern day Test cricketer regarding the financial rewards which are finally coming his way. Nor, in fact, do I believe that we were particularly hard done by. Others may have a right to feel differently, but despite its ups and downs my personal cricket life and subsequent involvement in the game have been most rewarding in so many ways. No more so than now, when I am privileged to see every home Test match and every other game of major consequence from the greatest of vantage points.

Possibly the one match in the period of time covering my television work to give the greatest satisfaction from every possible angle also took place at Trent Bridge. I refer to England v Australia in 1977. The Jubilee Test at Lords had been drawn, victory had come our way at Old Trafford and excitement in the possible downfall of the old enemy had reached fever pitch when the teams arrived in Nottingham. Consider also the possibilities surrounding this great occasion.

Her Majesty The Queen at Trent Bridge on the first day of the Test match in 1977 being introduced to the England players by captain Mike Brearley.

1. There was a distinct opportunity for England to record their first Test victory over Australia on this ground for 47 years.

2. It heralded the return of England's finest batsman, Geoff Boycott, after a self-imposed absence of three years.

3. Local hero Derek Randall was to make his first Test match appearance on his home ground.

4. It marked the Test debut of Somerset's rising star, 21-year-old Ian Botham.

5. Jeff Thomson, the scourge of England in Australia, was again striking peak form.

6. Her Majesty The Queen was to grace Trent Bridge on the very first day as part of the Silver Jubilee celebrations.

Our prayers for a spell of sunny weather were answered and with one exception the entire five days went as every Englishman hoped. The exception was poor Derek Randall being run out with his score on 13. Boycott announced his return to the Test match arena with scores of 107 and 80 not out and had the singular experience of batting on all five days. Ian Botham began his Test career with five first innings wickets and Jeff Thomson bowled superbly but with very little luck. Victory came England's way soon after tea on the fifth day and it was appropriate that Randall made the winning hit after his unfortunate first innings.

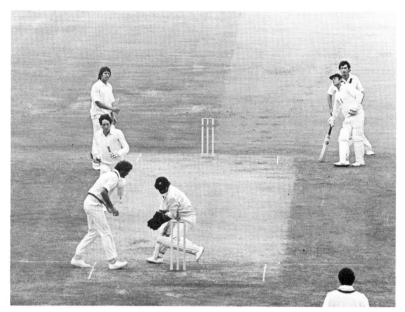

Over 20,000 highly satisfied spectators clocked in on each of the first four days and another 8,000 on the final day led to receipts amounting to £152,000, the biggest figure ever for a match outside London and £80,000 more than the previous best at Trent Bridge. If it all added up to a superb game of cricket, enhanced by the magnificent organisation of the Nottinghamshire Committee. Few people are aware of the work involved in presenting a five-day Test match and the Committee left nothing undone.

I mentioned at the start of this chapter the friendliness and comradeship which has always existed on this historic ground. There has always been a warm welcome for all with hospitality second to none. I could not conclude without a special reference to the Trent Bridge crowd. There has been growing concern in recent seasons about the noise and rowdiness which prevails on many of our grounds, principally caused by the bars being open all day long. For those who derive real and genuine enjoyment from the game of cricket, it has been particularly upsetting. The behaviour of the packed crowds at Trent Bridge was exemplary and, more than that, the manner of their applause showed them to be experts in their judgement of the game. So enthusiastic did they become that they even welcomed the players in and out from the practice sessions.

It is a long time now since Nottinghamshire supporters have had very much to cheer about, yet surprisingly only Yorkshire and Surrey have won more Championship titles. For many of us who have been privileged to experience the great joy of many unforgettable days at Trent Bridge future successes for Nottinghamshire cannot come too quickly.

Edgbaston

It would be wrong to complete my round up of our Test match grounds without including Edgbaston, though as a player it was the one I knew least of all. Very often Surrey's Warwickshire fixture would clash with a Test match and on least two occasions Surrey, in the nicest possible way, were sent to Coventry. Thus it was that I appeared for the County only twice, once in 1950 and then again nine years later a few weeks prior to my retirement. In between there was a Test Trial and my two Test appearances: in 1957 v West Indies and the following year v New Zealand. A check on my personal performances in those few appearances would, I am sure, prove to be more than embarrassing and certainly I have derived far more satisfaction in my many visits to Edgbaston as a BBC commentator.

The transformation which has taken place in Birmingham in 30 years has been a major success story in terms of post-war English cricket. The expert manner in which the Warwickshire Club and their Supporters Association arranged a mammoth weekly football pool laid the foundations for a vast capital income, all of which has been ploughed back into making Edgbaston the most complete of our Test match grounds. The playing area is completely encircled by a terraced embankment with full seating accommodation, with better vantage points for watching the game than anywhere I know.

Above: Alvin Kallicharran batting for West Indies against England. In recent seasons he has batted well for Warwickshire. *Previous page:* The terraces at Edgbaston. Since the war, the Warwickshire Club, enormously helped by the Supporters Association, has built Edgbaston into one of the best-appointed grounds in the world.

50

Fellow off-spinner Lance Gibbs bowled for Warwickshire for many years, and recently overhauled Freddie Trueman's record number of Test match wickets.

Luxury abounds in the many and varied private function rooms and ladies have their own stand accommodation and refreshment facilities. Most important, the players have not been forgotten. Practice can be undertaken on good grass pitches, artificial wickets and, when bad weather interferes, in the excellent Indoor School. Parking lots are varied and substantial and the Press, Radio and Television have been particularly well catered for. Our own TV commentary position is always behind the bowler's arm, at exactly the right height, in a large and comfortable carpeted room.

It would be hard to visualise this magnificent stadium anywhere else than in the city of Birmingham. Everything about it reeks of the prosperity of this great centre of industry. Yet there has always been one major worry. I have always sensed a great indifference towards cricket from Birmingham's vast population, which inevitably has left the Edgbaston ground too often deserted. Even on Test match days it is a rarity to see the place more than two-thirds occupied. Soccer remains the great love of the Midlands with three major clubs, Aston Villa, Birmingham City and West Bromwich Albion in the near vicinity and Wolverhampton Wanderers not too far away.

Many believe that the locals demand success before they will give their support for any professional club and on the face of it Warwickshire CCC have worked desperately hard to produce a match-winning combination but with little significant success. With the advent of overseas players and the ready supply of cash at their disposal they went overboard in their efforts to attract the top names to Edgbaston. At one stage, in Kanhai, Kallicharan, Murray and Gibbs they had a third of the great West Indian side in their ranks. Add to these a fine trio of English batsmen in Amiss, Jameson and Mike Smith and you would not believe that any other county side could live with them, particularly in limited-over cricket. It is 11 years since they won the Gillette Cup and to date they have drawn a blank in both Benson and Hedges and John Player competitions. As for the County Championship, they have had one solitary success in the last 27 years.

Although my experience of league and club cricket in the area is limited, I have always been under the impression that the standard is as high as anywhere in the country – yet there is a dearth of talent making its way into first class cricket. Possibly there are two reasons for this. There cannot be much incentive for the promising colt who finds himself in instant competition for a place in the side with established overseas stars. Secondly in a city such as Birmingham there must be great opportunities in commerce and business which would offer greater financial rewards and security than would cricket. Perhaps cricket's new pay structure will prove to be a new bait. Now for instance one can safely say that the chances of, for instance, Bob Willis exceeding £20,000 a year are very good and

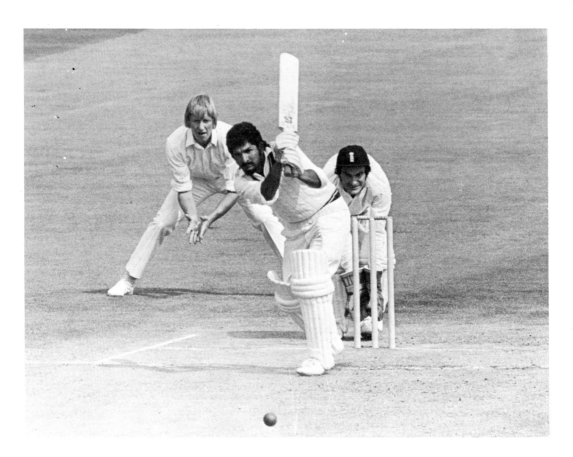

this in itself must help in attracting young players into the game. Let us hope so for Warwickshire deserve success on the field to match the hard work that has established Edgbaston as a super stadium.

Historically the ground will for ever be remembered for two quite sensational performances in the early 1920s. It was in 1922 when Warwickshire, batting first, made 223 and then proceeded to bowl Hampshire out for 15. Following on, the visitors in their second innings confounded everyone by amassing a total in excess of 500 and followed that by dismissing Warwickshire for 158 to record one of the most remarkable victories of all time by a margin of 155 runs. Two years later, in a Test Match, the Sussex combination of Arthur Gilligan and Maurice Tate wrote their names in the record books by bowling out South Africa for 30, a total which included 11 extras! Gilligan 6 for 7, Tate 4 for 12 were their astonishing figures. The entire innings lasted only 45 minutes – impossible these days.

More recently I look back to 1957 when Edgbaston became the ground where Sonny Ramadhin, after torturing English batsmen for seven long years, was finally mastered thanks to the efforts of May and Cowdrey. He was never the same bowler again. It was also here that Zaheer Abbas, in his first Test Match against England,

Left: Deryck Murray, wicket-keeper of West Indies, and another of the players from the Caribbean to help Warwickshire. Deryck is batting in this picture, with Alan Knott keeping and Frank Hayes at slip.
Right: One of the best Test match innings seen in recent years at Edgbaston was the first appearance of Zaheer Abbas against England. He made a magnificent 274.

made a brilliant 274, an innings full of driving of the highest quality.

Sadly there are also memories of a different kind. The refusal of Arthur Fagg to continue umpiring in the West Indies Test, the unhappy demise of the unfortunate Denness as England's captain and the blatant piece of intimidation executed by Bob Willis at Pakistan bowler Quasim, who could only boast a Test Match batting of three, linger in the mind. Fortunately the happier days at Edgbaston remain more firmly in memory. None more so than the 12.30 ritual on Test match days when that great host Cyril Goodway fights his way through the maze of seats and spectators carrying a large tray of assorted beverages for the Radio and Television commentary teams. On no other Test match ground in the world do you get this kind of service from the chairman of the Club. May it long continue.

Headingley

It was the summer of 1932 when I first set foot inside the Headingley cricket ground in Leeds. Yorkshire were playing Nottinghamshire and Hedley Verity took all 10 wickets at a cost of only 10 runs. Such a performance was wasted on my tender years, but two years later I was just about able to appreciate my first sight of Don Bradman, when I sat quietly and spellbound as the 'Master' made 304 against England. I never saw him again until he walked quickly past me in the gully at Kennington Oval in 1948, took guard and made 146 at 50 runs per hour. Infrequent visits followed at Headingley, for the simple reason that Park Avenue was so much nearer home and in truth one felt much closer to the action on the compact Bradford ground.

My first real association with Headingley began in the winter of 1937/38 when my mother strained her resources to book me a series of practice-cum-coaching lessons at Herbert Sutcliffe's Winter School. In those days the practice sheds were sited where the present pavilion stands and the then players' pavilion has since been converted to committee rooms. Practice began at 1 pm on Saturday throughout the winter, and as I arrived at the main entrance for the first time ever, I enquired where I should find the changing rooms. The directions I was given led me to the changing rooms of the Leeds Rugby League Club and before I could say 'knife' I was in the midst of men I had not seen the like of before, reeking of embrocation but enjoying the joke to the full. I became a convert to Leeds rugby, as our cricket sessions ended just in time to allow me to watch the second half on the adjoining ground. For 40 years I have remained a fan and even now can recall, as though it were yesterday, the great Jim Brough at full back, the electrifying speed of Australian Eric Harris on the wing, the brilliance of Stanley Brogden in the centre. Two superb half backs were the Welshman Jenkins and the mighty Vic Hey at stand off, and the enormous Jubb remained my favourite forward.

Back at the indoor school the coaching was in the hands of Ben Wilson, a Yorkshire pre-1914 opener and the one and only Emmott Robinson. Emmott was the personification of Yorkshire cricket. For him it was a way of living. He was a terribly serious man, any humour being completely unconscious, yet more words of cricket wisdom came from those lips than from anyone I have ever met. I purposely changed back from my whites in the slowest possible time, in the hope of catching more pearls of wisdom.

On two or three occasions I was lucky enough to leave the ground with him and share a penny tram ride back to Leeds city centre. I cannot believe I uttered a word but sat enthralled listening to his reminiscences. Right out of the blue, a few years later Emmott wrote to me when I had been in the Middle East for a couple of years. Regrettably I lost the letter somewhere in Egypt, for it was a classic.

In my first visit to Headingley I saw Hedley Verity take 10 wickets for 10 runs. I was too young to claim that it was this inspired performance that persuaded me to be a slow bowler.

Previous page: Headingley 40 years after my first visit, with England playing Australia.

Don Bradman in his heyday in the 1930s. As a boy I saw his magnificent 304 at Headingley in 1934, and next saw him when he scored 146 at the Oval in 1948 – I was one of the bowlers he hit to all corners of the ground.

Three pages of solid cricket news and not a punctuation mark from start to finish.

I suppose I showed a fair amount of promise around that time, but I was certainly nothing out of the ordinary and it came as a surprise when I had a postcard from Jack Nash, the Yorkshire secretary, inviting me to join the Colts and attend at Spring nets with the Yorkshire cricketers. The postcard remains among my souvenirs and is proof of my first remuneration from the game of cricket. I was paid ten shillings and my tram fare.

That I had reached this stage was mainly due to one person who played the leading part in my cricket education and without whose enthusiasm, generosity and great friendship I would have remained but a useful league cricketer. Harry Dolphin, nephew of the Yorkshire wicket-keeper, was 12 years my senior yet when I was between 15 and 20 we were the closest of friends. By profession he was a freelance journalist, but he did only sufficient work to provide

57

himself with the necessities of life, and the rest of his time revolved around the game of cricket. He read about it avidly and studied the game from every angle. A non-smoker and teetotaller, he also had a dreaded fear of any female entanglement which could interfere with his cricket. He was a prolific wicket-taker in club cricket with a mixture of leg spin, top spin and googlies and no matter what the occasion there would always be a cricket ball in his pocket. The two of us played together at every conceivable opportunity. I recall him receiving £2 for a small piece in the *Bradford Telegraph & Argus*, and racing round to my house with two ten-shilling cheap day return tickets to London for the following day. We left Bradford station at 7 am complete with bat, ball and stumps and arrived just on midday at Kings Cross. A bus took us straight to Hyde Park, where the two of us pitched the stumps and played solidly through until we returned to Bradford on the early evening train. Little wonder everyone thought us quite crazy. I bade farewell to Harry prior to embarking on a troopship to Egypt. He was crestfallen thinking what Hitler had done to his beloved game. Twelve months later he wrote to me saying he too was in the Army, had volunteered for overseas and was on his way to join me. The plan was never fulfilled for a week out of England his ship was torpedoed and sunk without trace. It was one of the unhappiest days of my life.

My association with Headingley and Yorkshire cricket was resumed with Australia's memorable victory at Leeds in 1948 where I shouldered the main responsibility for England's defeat. Without wishing to offer too many excuses I believe, on reflection, that as a highly inexperienced Test player with less than 12 months first-class

I myself received some hints from that great character of Yorkshire cricket, immortalised by Neville Cardus and others, Emmott Robinson. Here he is putting me through my paces. The youngster to my right, Johnny Lawrence, later played for Somerset.

cricket, the occasion proved too much for me. The atmosphere was electric, with attendance figures of 158,000 and many thousands turned away. The attendance remains and indeed is likely to remain, a record for a Test Match in this country.

Of one point I am certain – Headingley to this day is not an easy ground on which to bowl. The slope from the Kirkstall Lane end down towards the football stand requires a good deal of experience to negotiate and many have discovered that it is the easiest thing in the world to lose one's rhythm on the approach to the wicket. In common with many bowlers I much preferred to come in from the football end. Years ago, during a hot spell, the wicket was as easy as any in the land on which to bat, and the outfield became lightning fast with the ball racing to the edge like a marble on a skating rink. For all that there was no way in which Australia should have scored

59

404 for 3 on the fifth and final day in 1948. The selectors had erred in picking only one spin bowler and the wear and tear on the pitch around the leg stump cried out for a leg break bowler. Despite another Bradman hundred it was left-hander Arthur Morris with a brilliant 182 who made victory possible. The rough around his off stump was made for me to destroy him and Neil Harvey, which would have made an English victory certain, but I failed hopelessly to take advantage of it. A few years later that great Australian side would have done well to have reached 200. Since that fateful day 30 years ago hardly a year has gone by without my returning to Headingley in some capacity or other and it would take a book in itself to recall the dramas and stirring events which have taken place there. Memorable bowling performances by Trueman, Loader, Underwood and Gilmour, a triple hundred from the bat of John Edrich, Boycott's great day in achieving his hundreth century and the desecration of the Test pitch, are only a few of many noteworthy events.

I mentioned earlier what a first class batting surface one could always expect there but in recent seasons it has become impossible to predict what a batsman may now find. A good wicket has become the exception rather than the rule. On some occasions Arnold and Old have moved the ball off the pitch like spin bowlers, while on others the wicket-keeper has taken successive balls of identical length, one shoulder high and the next by his ankles. The wicket produced for the Roses match of 1978 was a 'frightener' and the game ended in a day and a half.

At least the big crowd that continues to flock down St Michaels Lane if they feel that there is half a chance of a real contest has never changed. The enthusiasm and appetite for the game is unchanged and unsatiable. In my eyes Headingley spectators remain the most knowledgeable in England and personally I have never received anything but the friendliest of welcomes from them.

I am not so convinced that the same applies to the Yorkshire Committee, although of course in common with one or two others who went elsewhere to seek fame (if not fortune) I and my views have been regarded with a good deal of suspicion. There has in fact been a history of disagreements between players and Committee, and over the years such names as Wardle, Trueman, Illingworth, Close and Boycott have at times made headline news in this respect. As recently as last summer I heard a prominent member of the Yorkshire Committee openly expressing the hope that Brearley would make Test match runs to ensure that his own county captain would be deprived of the job of leading England.

There are, of course, some excellent members of the Committee with a shrewd understanding of the game, but there have been far too many others who should never have been allowed near a

Committee meeting. When I was a youth working in Barclays Bank in Bradford, the district manager was a certain Algernon Denham, who subsequently became chairman of the Halifax Building Society. On requesting permission for an afternoon off to play in a Yorkshire Colts trial, I was rebuked by Mr Denham and given a stern lecture on the foolishness of wasting my time chasing a cricket ball when I was fortunate enough to have secured a position in his bank. 'Forget the cricket and stick to the job' were his final words. Several years later I arrived at Headingley to play in a Test match and just about the first person I bumped into was Mr Denham, now a fully fledged member of the Yorkshire Committee. 'I am delighted you have done so well, I always felt you had the making of a fine cricketer,' he said. I believe I could be excused for totally ignoring him. A brilliant business man he may well have been, but his knowledge of cricket was infinitesimal.

The Yorkshire Committee have now gone through a long period of frustration as it is 11 years since the Championship has come their way, not good enough for a county which for 115 years has dominated our cricket with 31 championship successes.

For eight of those eleven years Geoffrey Boycott has been captain and consequently he has been severely criticised. When he took over in 1972 Yorkshire played 17 games in succession without a victory and suffered their worst-ever season finishing in 13th position. What their fate would have been without Boycott is hard to imagine. He scored over 2,000 runs, averaged an incredible 109.85 and became the first Englishman ever to finish with a three-figure batting average. The performances of his colleagues were abysmal. Yorkshire cricket struck rock bottom, and if Sir Donald Bradman, A.B. Sellars or Stuart Surridge had been skipper, I cannot for a moment believe that the results Yorkshire achieved would have been very much better.

Perhaps Boycott has lacked several vital qualifications necessary for a successful captain as for a long time cricket for him revolved solely around G. Boycott, though I believe his views now have slowly began to widen. He has possibly lacked a certain flair, imagination, understanding and compassion and his team mates have found it difficult to strike any real alliance or friendship with him. He is a loner, though not these days through his own choice. Tactically he is first class, and is a deep thinker particularly on the finer points of the game, where he has impressed us all by his assessments on television.

I thought he was particularly ill-treated when the Brearley or Boycott as captain controversy was at its height. Instead of trying to extol the virtues of Brearley as a captain, and there was endless scope for them to do this, many people delivered an out-and-out attack on Boycott, both as a man and as a captain, which I believed was thoroughly unjustified and in very bad taste. The pressures on a captain in Yorkshire are possibly greater than anywhere else and with the players at his disposal, Boycott has been on a hiding to nothing.

It has taken too long in many people's eyes for the long awaited improvement in the county of the White Rose but there are now definite signs of light in the dark tunnel. The County Committee made a grave error in dispensing with Raymond Illingworth's services and their decision to recall him as a cricket manager is a step in the right direction. With youngsters such as Sharp, Athey and all-rounder Stevenson looking more like the heroes of old, the return of Yorkshire cricket to its accustomed position of the 1960s is likely to come sooner rather than later.

One of Yorkshire's best hopes for an early revival to their traditional greatness. Bill Athey shows something of Boycott's determination not to be out as he comes forward, straight bat, eye on the ball, no gap between bat and pad – as it says on his bat (from my old friend Stuart Surridge): perfect.

Lord's

Unless there are extenuating circumstances a cricketer is normally first aware that he has been selected to play in a Test if he should happen to switch on the radio news. An official letter follows within 24 hours laying down the 'do's and don'ts', but in my time there was no entrance ticket to the ground enclosed. I was first selected for a Test match at Lord's in 1948 and reported for practice, as is the custom, at 3 pm the previous day. In those days I could neither afford to buy a car or even rent one, so I had humped my great cricket bag across London via the Underground and buses. As a single man living in 'digs' in South London, I took advantage of the hotel accommodation reserved at the Great Western Hotel in Paddington and on the morning of the match made my own way up to Lord's around 10.15 am. As I walked proudly through the Grace gates I was stopped abruptly in my tracks by two officials demanding my entrance ticket. There was no reason why they should recognise me and the same applied to a group of nearby onlookers. Furthermore I only received a wry smile when I gave my name. The gentlemen were far from convinced, and I was getting desperate. My salvation arrived in the shape of Mr Martin, the Lord's groundsman, who remembered me taking a hiding from Denis Compton the previous year.

Leslie Ames in his Test playing days. After the war he was the first professional to become a full-time selector.
Previous page: The headquarters of cricket. Lord's is a lovely ground, with an atmosphere all its own, but there are things I would like to see changed.

My experience, however, did not compare to that of poor George Emmett who was twelfth man during that Test match. He was detained for a full 15 minutes. On offering his name and status he was sharply told to clear off as three George Emmetts had already gone in. Times have not changed a great deal and even to this day I continue to have problems with gate officials at each and every entrance. In most other respects Lord's has changed a good deal and thankfully for the better, though I believe three major items should have some consideration.

The standard of wickets at a ground universally claimed to be the headquarters of cricket has fallen appreciably in recent years and a reassessment of the whole square should be undertaken. I cannot speak of pre-war Lord's pitches but certainly in the 1940s and early 1950s they were a good deal better than they are today. It would have been totally impossible for Compton and Edrich between them to score 7,355 runs in a season in 1978. Good batsmen are those who quickly assess the length and bounce of a ball and put themselves in a position to play a shot. Too many Lord's wickets have given such a variance in pace and bounce recently as to make batting not only a lottery but at times distinctly hazardous.

Having offered this criticism let me absolve any blame from groundsman Jim Fairbrother. You could search long and hard to find a better practitioner or indeed a more conscientious man. There has always been too much cricket played at Lord's and once the summer is under way the ground staff find themselves with

Above: George Emmett. Because Lord's didn't issue tickets to Test match players, he couldn't get in.
Above right: A traditional match at Lord's, dating back to the days of W.G. Grace, and only recently abolished, was Gentlemen v Players. This is a Players side in my days. *Left to right, back:* Fred Gardner, D.V. Smith, Tom Graveney, Fred Trueman, Dick Richardson, Tom Clark. *Front:* Frank Tyson, Godfrey Evans, Denis Compton, Eric Hollies, myself.

precious few free days to work on the square itself. For years Sunday was a free day, but the advent of Sunday cricket and still more wickets to prepare gives the ground staff an unenviable task. In September of each year at most grounds one can see the ends of all pitches being dug up and re-turfing and re-seeding taking place. My contention is that a cricket pitch will not last for ever, and remember that we have been playing on these same strips for 100 years or more. They have been pounded and battered year in and year out and many have lost their resilience and are worn out. There must surely be a case after all this time for a completely new square to be relaid over a period of two seasons. With modern science and technique Kerry Packer proved it possible to prepare wickets in just a few weeks and those produced are apparently excellent wickets.

The press box and the television commentary box housed at the top of the Warner stand is both comfortable and roomy. For the casual visitor it gives a birds-eye view of the whole scene, and provided one does not wish to concentrate too much on the events in the middle it is an admirable spot to enjoy a day's cricket. For the professional cricket writer, who might be keen to inform his million readers whether Joe Bloggs missed a perfectly straight ball or was on the receiving end of something just about unplayable, the day can be full of frustration. Just as a batsman should have the right to bat on a good pitch, a press man should be able to watch and report on the game from the only true position – behind the bowler's arm. The long and narrow top balcony of the Lord's pavilion would be the ideal position. From a television viewpoint I am frequently asked if I watch the cricket or do commentary strictly from the monitor alongside me. Instinctively, a cricketer who moves on to television will watch the live action. Years in the middle give him a cricket brain and a trained eye to look for a set of circumstances unknown to those without that experience. Quick as he might be to assess an over, ball by ball, he would be completely at a loss if he were to attempt this at Lord's, from a position over deep extra cover. It remains vital to concentrate on the monitor, which usually gives a picture smaller and inferior to the larger set at home. To a degree this puts one in the the hands of the cameraman. Thankfully they make few mistakes, but like everyone they are human and you live in fear of missing a catch or some important incident out of range. A day's commentary at Lord's leaves one fairly drained.

My third criticism of Lord's is that it is surely time that MCC followed the line of many counties and gave more serious consideration to the ladies. It seems to me that year by year they are forming an increasing percentage of our cricket watching crowd, they support the game equally as well as their male counterparts, are equally enthusiastic, infinitely better behaved and smarter in appearance – and they deserve equal rights. Is it not strange that so many who object to seeing a woman set foot inside the Long Room at Lord's will vote for a lady to be Prime Minister.

Having dispensed my three criticisms in what I hope is a constructive manner, let me say that to play cricket at Lord's for the contracted cricketer is a far happier experience in modern times than it ever was for our forefathers. It is my view that cricket has done more to move with the times than any other sport, and this has meant more radical changes being made in the character and organisation of cricket at Lord's than anyone could possibly have imagined. Of course in the very early days when the country as a whole was either rich or poor, it had to be the upper classes who governed the game of cricket. In the period between the two wars a new generation of cricketers appeared on the scene. They were top class professionals and numbered in their ranks were such names as Leslie Ames, Alf Gover and Hedley Verity, cricketers sufficiently well educated, without reaching University standards, to achieve success both on and off the field. For all that there was little chance of their breaking through the solid amateur barrier which continued to dominate the Lord's scene. There was always a certain amount of tension and a good deal of pressure even in the early post-war years when one played at headquarters. One could not fail to notice the differential which still existed between the amateur and the professional, but by the early 1950s several quite startling changes were taking place. Len Hutton became the first professional captain of England and later was the first professional cricketer to be elected as an MCC member while still playing. Leslie Ames became the first professional appointed as a full-time selector.

Boris Karloff was a great cricket lover and thought a visit to the player's dressing rooms at Lord's was like going to Heaven. I was invited to America to be on his 'This is Your Life' programme, from which this picture is taken.

Freddie Laker, myself and John Pennell at Gatwick Airport. Fred and I frequently exchange correspondence, as I get asked for airline tickets while he gets asked for autographs by young cricket lovers.

Simultaneously came an appointment extremely well received by cricketers in all walks of life. In 1952 'Billy' Griffith was made Assistant Secretary of MCC, a position he occupied for 10 years before taking over the Secretaryship from Ronnie Aird. I do not believe I met a truer amateur cricketer than Billy Griffith. He had toured West Indies with me in 1947-48 and the total expenses he received for four months in the Caribbean were £25. He was a kindly, courteous and compassionate man, whose manner would not differ if he were addressing the President of MCC or a beggar boy in the back streets of Jamaica. He had sufficient foresight to see that changes had to take place at Lord's and it was during his period of office that the platforms were built which these days ensure that the ground has become friendlier and warmer. People and personalities from all walks of life have been drafted in not only as MCC members but also to play leading roles as Committee members. Who knows, maybe one year Alec Bedser will become President. Alec along with Ken Barrington and Charlie Elliott are at the moment our selectors, all of them respected former professionals. But it would be wrong to conclude that this particular door is now firmly closed to anyone from Oxford or Cambridge. 'Gubby' Allen, like most of us, has his detractors but in my time there was no better selector. He was an extremely good judge of a player and his potential and would not be swayed by a one-off performance on the eve of a selector's meeting but stuck firmly to the player of class. He made fewer errors than most.

On the question of selling the game of cricket to the public, in fact on sponsorship as a whole, the greatest stride forward has been made. Perhaps it took a little while to persuade many of the old diehards that the Gillette Cup was a worthwhile venture. Once this point had been proved there followed the John Player League, the Benson and Hedges Cup, the Prudential Trophy, the Schweppes County Championship and more recently the Cornhill Test Matches. Sixteen years have now passed since the first negotiations were completed on commercially backed cricket and not one major withdrawal has taken place. Compare that with the records of golf and tennis and one can only come to the conclusion that the excellence of MCC's Public Relations and Sponsorship Committees has been the prime cause in retaining substantial financial investment by these highly regarded companies.

The facilities offered in the Tavern boxes are second to none on any cricket ground. Lord's still makes a great impact on so many visitors and I shall always cherish the remarks of our old friend, now long departed, actor Boris Karloff. On first being taken into the players' dressing room and escorted on to our small balcony, he gazed out upon the scene and with just a hint of that dreaded lisp he turned and said 'This is just like dying and going into Heaven'.

Tony Lock

As a schoolboy I idolised Hedley Verity. As a Test cricketer I would put Johnny Wardle in the highest category. As a commentator I never ceased to marvel at the performances of Derek Underwood. They all, of course, have a common factor as they all bowled left arm leg breaks. Brilliant exponents of the art they might have been, but I would not have exchanged any one of them for my regular Surrey and England partner over a period of eleven years, Graham Anthony Richard Lock.

In so many ways we were poles apart and sometimes it is hard to recall what on earth we ever had in common. Tony was seven and a half years my junior and a 17-year-old and a 25-year-old have strangely different views. He was a country lad and played in the leisurely atmosphere of the lovely Oxted Cricket Club, watched over by a doting father. On the other hand I had emerged from the industrial north, endured the rigours of tough league cricket and been fatherless since the age of two. I had completed nearly five years active service abroad almost before Tony left school. Not surprisingly, in the early days we were never close friends, although there were never any serious arguments between us. On away trips we invariably went our different ways in the evenings. Tony would sort out a local cinema whilst I would normally be found talking cricket in an hotel bar.

Once on the cricket field everything changed, and I would take a lot of convincing that as a spinning combination we ever had any serious rivals. Together we captured 4,788 wickets in first-class cricket, 367 of those in our 95 Test matches. We were both prodigious spinners of a cricket ball, which usually meant we could get a modicum of turn on wickets unresponsive to the average bowler. Consequently on a helpful pitch we could increase our pace which cut down the prospects of batsmen attempting to get after us. It is seldom that you find a batsman equally at home against the ball spinning on to him plus the one turning from leg. For example, Denis Compton and Doug Insole were superb players of off spin and both would have scored more heavily against me had it not been for Tony at the other end. In contrast Sir Len Hutton and Don Kenyon would play left-arm leg spin till the cows came home, yet I had a high success rate against them. In every way then it was an

ideal partnership thought it is only fair to say that Tony was of greater
help to me than I was to him, due to his brilliance in the leg trap. I
have no idea how many batsman departed 'caught Lock, bowled
Laker'. It was rumoured that the compositor in the Oval printing
shop kept the line constantly made up.

The story of Tony Lock's cricket career is indeed a most
remarkable one. I first recall him as a well-made youngster of 16, a
head full of red hair, with a quiff falling over his eyes.

As far as I can remember the first time we played together was in
a second eleven game at Bristol early in 1947. He was a slow flighty
bowler and bowled with little or no spin to a deep extra cover and a
long off. The Gloucester wicket at Bristol that year had had the sand
treatment and was made for the finger spinner. Monty Cranfield
tore through us with nine cheap wickets which seemed to suggest
that I was in for a hatful. Indeed the ball spun at right angles and for

the first time I had G.A.R. Lock at short leg. It is not an exaggeration to say that in the first hour he dropped four catches! I looked at the crestfallen youngster and said to our skipper the Hon. R.R. Blades 'Do the kid a favour and stick him on the boundary, he will never be a short leg as long as he plays the game'. Not one of my most prophetic remarks and one that Lockie and I have enjoyed for years. Within a year Tony had gone away to do his National Service and I saw little of him but noticed he had collected his fair share of wickets in Services cricket without any of the devastating performances that came later.

On his return to the Oval he made regular appearances in 1949 and was capped the following summer. Yet Tony had a problem. I mentioned earlier that his style was that of the old fashioned orthodox left arm spinner; Wilfred Rhodes and Jack White spring to mind. He would look to deceive batsmen in the air and his line was off stump and outside with a packed off-side field. Around that time we played on several rain affected pitches when Tony was all at sea with his method of bowling while at the other end I was regularly snapping up five, six or seven cheap wickets. Consequently we discussed the idea of improving his power of spin and increasing his pace, and at the end of the season we quietly spent some time together in the nets working on a new grip for him, very similar to the one I employed.

I disappeared overseas that winter and Tony, determined to succeed with a different method, took himself off to Allders Indoor Cricket School in Croydon and for hours every day throughout the long winter he worked diligently on his bowling. There was one terrible snag. The net at Allders was not sufficiently high for a full extension of the arm at the point of delivery and a tall bowler giving the ball even the slightest degree of height was seriously restricted. As a result Tony increased his delivery stride to almost that of a fast bowler, thus reducing the height at which he released the ball, and to make doubly sure of no net interference his left arm was slightly bent at the elbow.

None of the Surrey players were aware of those events that winter and when we all returned to the Oval in April we could only stare in amazement as Tony joined the practice sessions. The net wickets, due to rain, were far from satisfactory and as he ran in and let the ball go at near medium pace, he made it turn and kick. Jack Parker looked at me and said 'He will never get away with it'. I was not quite so sure that his delivery was illegal but it was certainly very close to the mark. He would certainly have been banned in present times. There has never been anything illegal about bowling with a bent or crooked arm, provided it remains that way until after the ball is released. It contravenes the rules only when the arm is straightened prior to delivery which then constitutes a jerk or a

Tony's action in 1953, a picture taken when his selection for the West Indies tour was announced. It was in the West Indies that Tony was eventually called for throwing.

72

throw. Tony's quicker deliveries certainly fell into the latter category, but I never agreed with the opinion of many that he was an out and out 'chucker'.

In a strange way his new action improved my own bowling, for on wickets which helped the spinner the boot now was on the other foot. For a period I was the one being left behind and had to pull out all the stops to prevent being well beaten in what became an annual race for 100 wickets. Tony remained aloof to the many sarcastic and cynical remarks from opposing batsmen. As the quicker ones thumped into Arthur McIntyre's gloves before Keith Miller was half way through his shot, the Australian responded with 'strike one'! Doug Insole left the crease with his middle stump flattened with the words 'I agree, I am out but was I bowled or run out?' In disposing of George Headley in Jamaica, Tony left only one stump standing and the shattered Headley passed me at mid wicket saying 'Dis ain't cricket, man, dis is war'.

It was in fact in the West Indies when Tony was eventually no-balled for throwing. The keen Barbados crowd had spotted the irregularity ahead of any one else and immediately dubbed him 'Shylock'. The no-ball call was an afterthought by umpire Walcott, for Tony had already bowled a youthful Sobers with a quick one and Gary had removed his gloves and was on his way back before the roar of 'no ball' came from square leg. Suitably encouraged Walcott repeated the call a couple of balls later and his partner Jordan took similar action when Lock changed ends. He did not bowl the faster ball again. Apart from these problems in the West Indies I can only recall one English umpire taking such drastic steps. A courageous Fred Price was given a hard time by the Oval crowd, and one felt a good deal of sympathy for a man who was conscientiously doing his job. So the years drifted on and nobody seriously suggested that Tony should change his style though a lot of murmur came from Lock's arch rival Johnny Wardle of Yorkshire, who in fairness was missing his share of international caps.

The rivalry between these two was intense, never more so than when they were in direct opposition. I suppose that Johnny came off the better of the two during their many confrontations, the most memorable of which occurred in Johnny's benefit match at Bradford when Surrey were the visitors. As fate would have it, Tony was bowling when Johnny came in to bat to receive the traditional 'one off the mark'. 'I don't really have to give *him* one, do I skipper' pleaded Tony and it was only after some persuasion that he grudgingly agreed. We all dropped back some 20 yards and Tony bowled a gift delivery. Johnny was going to make the most of this and pushed it quickly into the off side, raced down the pitch and kidded Tony by his call that he was taking two. Simultaneously Lock set off to do his own fielding and by the time his deadly left arm was about to go into action Wardle was leaning on his bat at the bowler's end doubled up with laughter. The two of them, in fact, only ever toured together once, when MCC visited South Africa in 1956/57. The tour was remarkable for a superb exhibition of wrist spin from Wardle, who exceeded 100 wickets and bowled magnificently. It was only in the final Test at Port Elizabeth when Johnny was injured that Tony made the Test side. Yet he came out of it all with a lot of credit. He was the first to appreciate Johnny's great talent, he bore no grudge, and was an ideal team man.

Tony and I made our one and only tour together to Australia under Peter May two years later. There he found that his style of bowling, so wonderfully effective in England, was blunted by the hard rock-like pitches down under. The medium-paced spinner is rarely effective under such conditions and this was certainly proved by his final Test figures of 5 for 376. Approaching his 30th birthday as the side arrived in New Zealand, it was a sadly disillusioned bowler who began to take stock of his career as he saw some film of his bowling one weekend. He had, in fact, unknowingly reached another turning point in his career. He was beset with a host of new problems. The film he saw gave positive proof that there was a kink in many instances at the point of delivery and this had to be rectified. He also had a thought at the back of his mind that he liked what he had seen of Australia. He very much wanted to play there again, yet he knew his present method was hardly likely to bring him the success he strived for. He came to think that if he changed his style of bowling, reverting to something between the slow flighty non-spinner of his early days and the lethal medium-paced jerk of the last few years, both his problems would be solved. Against this, he also had the nagging thought that he was due for a Surrey benefit the following year; could he therefore change his action once again yet have sufficient success to make his benefit season a good one financially.

The events of the next few years saw a remarkable change in the cricket life of G.A.R. Lock, events which he never could have visualized. In an incredibly short few months he once again reconstructed his action so well that he was ready to embark on a new career and to carry on for another ten years without a single objection to his bowling action.

The one major disappointment was his benefit year in 1960, when he was entitled to be thinking in terms of a five-figure sum. Just look at the benefits that had come the way of previous beneficaries:

1953	A. V. Bedser	£12,866	1957 E. D. W. Fletcher	£7,600
1955	A. J. McIntyre	£8,500	1958 E. R. Bedser	£7,700
1956	J. C. Laker	£11,000	1959 B. Constable	£6,515

Johnny Wardle, Tony Lock's chief rival for the left-arm spinner place in the England side. Quite different in style, they toured South Africa together in 1956-57, when Wardle was first choice. Each would have won more Test caps had the other not been around.

When the final count was made at the end of 1960 Tony's benefit realised a disappointing £4,700. Several of us had been extremely fortunate to cash in when Surrey were on the crest of a wave, but by the time Tony's year came round Surrey were on the decline. Yet one could argue that Surrey's record had not improved when Tom Clark and Ken Barrington followed with benefits worth £6,750 and £10,711 respectively.

It certainly exposed the frailties and unfairness of our benefit system. Thoroughly disenchanted and looking for pastures new, Tony recalled his enjoyment of Australia as a country and in the winter of 1962-63 he went out to Perth to play for Western Australia. Immediately successful and thoroughly enjoying the Australian way of life, he decided his future and that of his family lay in Perth, and after returning to fulfil the final year of his Surrey contract in 1963 he emigrated at the end of the summer and to all intents and purposes he was lost to English cricket for good.

If any Surrey player of the 1950s had drifted into the WACA ground in Perth during the next few years they would hardly have

credited that such a transformation in the person of G. A. R. Lock could ever have taken place. In contrast to the immature medium-paced spinner striving the whole time to pitch on the leg stump and hit the off, they would have seen the smooth flowing action of a genuine left-arm spinner, making intelligent use of the breeze, and capitalizing on his thoughtful study of batsmen's weaknesses. He was a cricketer with a complete understanding of the team which he now led, yet he retained the boyish enthusiasm which is a vital part of his make-up. The responsibility brought the best out of Tony and made him the complete cricketer.

Even in a magnificent Surrey fielding side, Tony Lock stood out. This diving attempt at a catch shows why. W.D. Davies of Glamorgan has played me round the corner and Tony is practically horizontal in mid-air as he stretches for it. Mickey Stewart, Arthur McIntyre and Ken Barrington watch.

He was in fact just what Western Australia badly needed. They had been on the verge of nearly breaking through to the top in Sheffield Shield cricket and were desperate to see Perth incorporated as a Test match venue. Both these targets were subsequently achieved and there can be little doubt that the country boy from Surrey played a leading part. He led the side to their run of success in Sheffield Shield cricket, became the leading wicket taker, spent uncountable hours developing the standard of young players and created a new atmosphere in Western Australian cricket.

If many people in England were unaware of these events on the other side of the world one person certainly was not. Mike Turner of Leicestershire, who for years has stood out for enterprise amongst our County secretaries, was hard at work trying to revitalise Leicestershire cricket and was shrewd enough to realise that Tony could help him to set the ball rolling. The thought of returning for the summer months to England, to captain a county side and to prove that at 36 he was still in the top flight of left-arm spinners, was a challenge he could not refuse, and in 1965 he signed a three-year contract with Leicestershire. Due to a previously agreed league contract he could play in only eight mid-week matches in 1965, but they served as a means of acquainting himself with the Leicestershire set up in addition to providing him with a further 35 wickets. He took over the side the following year, moved them up six places in the Championship table to eighth position and captured 109 wickets. In 1967 under his direction Leicestershire finished the season as runners-up to Yorkshire, the highest position they had ever achieved in their 88 years history, and the captain took 128 wickets at 18.11 apiece.

His enthusiasm was infectious and he led by example in every department of the game. He imbued the side with the belief that they were as good as any other and taught them never to give up hope. It is quite astonishing that in a short space of time he had worked the oracle with two sides 12,000 miles apart. A further season with Leicestershire became out of the question when he was suddenly beset with a number of domestic problems which demanded his staying in Perth. Yet even now he was not finally finished with English cricket. In a dramatic dash to the West Indies to reinforce Colin Cowdrey's touring side, he played in the last two Tests and at Georgetown shared a new record ninth wicket partnership of 109 with Pat Pocock to save the series. If I know my Tony, the 81 he made in Georgetown gave him more satisfaction than any bowling performance in any Test.

I have been questioned at regular intervals for 20 years how it was that when I took 19 for 90 against Australia on a helpful pitch, such a lethal left-hander as Tony could only manage 1 for 106. Of course he did not bowl as well as he might have done, but he had no luck whatsoever. Overcome with my own success at the time I must confess I omitted to consider how he must have felt. Since those days I have thought very often how I would have reacted if the boot had been on the other foot, as well it may have been. Now I appreciate how he has suffered for nobody has ever let him forget it.

After Tony's return from his last Test appearance, our ways unhappily did not cross for several years. The Centenary Test in Melbourne early in 1977 saw our partnership resumed for a memorable ten days; we even shared the same hotel room. Thirty years had passed since our first meeting and whereas in those early

A Surrey re-union in Perth for the second Test of the 1978-79 series. Ken Barrington (*right*) and I meet ex-Surrey players who have made Australia their home: Peter Loader, Ron Tindall, who also played football for, among others, Chelsea, and Tony Lock.

post-war years we seemed to have had precious little in common apart from a burning desire to take wickets, the passing years had brought us closer together, and our understanding and friendship is stronger now than at any other time.

Over a period of 25 years Tony Lock's career has not, in my view, ever been truly appreciated. He was just about the greatest competitor I ever saw, he never shirked an issue and never failed to give of his best. I have seen him bowl a 30-over spell with knees and ankles strapped up to such an extent that many would not have attempted to walk down the pavilion steps. He played a major part in Surrey's unique success story, he led Western Australia to win the Sheffield Shield, his inspiration saw Leicestershire away to the greatest decade in their history. He changed his style of bowling without ever losing its effectiveness. He had no peer as a short leg fieldsman and snapped up no less than 830 catches, a figure beaten only by F.E. Woolley and W.G. Grace. Add these to the 2,844 wickets he took at the low cost of 19.24, plus 10,336 runs with the bat, and his wonderful contribution to post-war cricket becomes clear.

I can only say it has been a privilege for me to have shared so many wonderful days with him and to have been part of a combination which, I hope, brought a good deal of enjoyment to a host of cricket followers.

Touring Overseas

Of the thousands of questions that are continually fired at all cricketers the one that is certainly the most difficult to answer relates to overseas tours. Which is the best and why? To anyone privileged to have visited every major cricketing country and also quite a number of lesser known cricketing fraternities, it is not a clear-cut decision. The answer and reasons for it will obviously vary according to the individual's likes and dislikes. One may relish the way of life in New Zealand, yet feel the cricket itself lacks that little something necessary to make it a true test of one's capabilities. The hospitality showered on touring cricketers when tours to South Africa were possible was second to none, yet many felt it difficult to come to terms with the political regime. However much batsmen enjoyed making runs in Bombay or Karachi there was always at the back of the mind the nagging problem of illness caused by a change of food and difficult living conditions.

Generally speaking, the vast majority of our players would plump unreservedly for a major tour to Australia. It is after all the highlight of a career. It combines a way of living which an Englishman can adapt to quite readily and a test of cricket at the highest level. The history of Anglo-Australian Test matches extends over 100 years, and it reveals how fortunate some Englishmen have been to have made the trip 'down under' and how many infinitely better players have retired without ever stepping out at Sydney or Melbourne.

For a long time I felt that I might fall into the latter category, having been passed over for Freddy Brown's tour in 1950-51 and again four years later when Len Hutton's side set sail. It is pointless now to go into the whys and wherefores of those selectors' decisions as that too is past history, but it did mean that I was into my 37th year before I was finally Australia-bound with an MCC side. This I found no hardship; in fact the experience of thousands of overs bowled in India, West Indies, South Africa and New Zealand had prepared me for the acid test, and my solitary tour to Australia was at least from a personal viewpoint highly successful.

Nowadays one feels that our present generation of tourists miss a great deal. Australian tours by popular demand have been cut almost in half with the curtailment of fixtures and the great advances in air travel. The old P & O or Orient line sailings from

80

Present-day tourists miss the camaraderie engendered by the long sea voyages, still an enjoyable part of cricket in my Test days. This jolly party consists of Colin Cowdrey, Godfrey Evans (part hidden), Tony Lock, Johnny Wardle, Trevor Bailey, Denis Compton, myself, Peter May, J.S. Bevan, Lord Rotherwick, Captain Farrow, Freddie Brown, Doug Insole, Peter Richardson, Brian Taylor, Alan Oakman, Frank Tyson, Peter Loader, Brian Statham, Jim Parks and George Duckworth.

London to Fremantle were an integral part of any tour. During those weeks it was possible to relax completely and recover from a rigorous English season. A fine team spirit was fostered and thoughts, ideas and tactics could be quietly worked out for the hard days which lay ahead. Acclimatisation came gradually from an early English autumn to the heat of an Australian summer. Now, of course, it is a day and a half huddled together in a jumbo jet, 2 or 3 days practice in the nets and immediately into the pressures of the modern game.

One of the greatest moments of my cricketing life was when I first set foot on Sydney Cricket Ground. Old enough to appreciate that I had finally reached the zenith of my cricket career, I recall to this very day taking the field that particular morning, momentarily closing my eyes and trying to soak up an atmosphere unrivalled on any other ground. A capacity house, glorious sunshine and two extraordinary fine sides in opposition; the realisation of a schoolboy's dream had finally materialised. My only disappointment came from the barrackers of the famous Hill. The passing years had not lessened the volume of their remarks, but it seemed to me there was a lack of wit and topicality. In fact any remark other than "Ave a go, ya mug' was something out of the ordinary. One

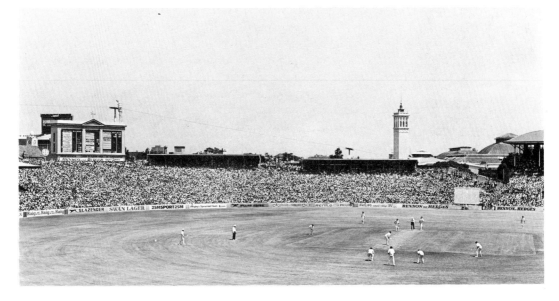

yearned for the return of the erstwhile Yabba who had kept not only the shirtless crowd around him totally amused throughout what can be a long and uncomfortable day, but had the players themselves in fits of laughter.

An uncomfortable day it certainly was when Hobbs and Sutcliffe defied everything that Australia could unleash at them and were still together at stumps. Naturally enough this great opening combination stole the backpage headlines in every Australian paper the following morning. The front pages told the story of an infamous abortionist, a certain nurse Reilly whose exploits had landed her in the High Court. Jack and Herbert carried on their partnership the following day to the utter frustration of another 60,000 onlookers. As the lunch break approached, the Yabba, who had apparently been contemplating the dire situation for some little time, burst into action. Raising himself to his full height, hands cupped round his mouth, he addressed himself to the Australian captain. 'Woodfull, why don't you send for nurse Reilly – she'll get the bastards out!'

Sadly in 1958-59 Sydney was allocated only one Test match but two Tests were played in Melbourne. It is probably heresy to say so but the home of Victorian cricket, to my way of thinking, lacks the atmosphere of Sydney, Lord's or Newlands at the Cape. It is a vast and magnificent stadium capable of accommodating something in excess of 100,000 people, and must be an ideal venue for an Australian Rules Final or indeed, as it was in 1956, for the Olympic Games. I never particularly enjoyed playing there, yet in common with every invited cricketer fortunate enough to be present for the 1977 Centenary Test match, I was overwhelmed with the magnificence of the occasion. Nowhere else in the world could the

Shipboard frolics. With sacks over our heads Peter May and I made a very respectable Tweedledum and Tweedledee.

organisation, the hospitality, and the many courtesies extended to all have been bettered. A book in itself would barely cover the story of those momentous ten days. Amongst the multitude of memories, I still cherish the sight of the perky 75-year old Eddie Paynter returning to Australia after an absence of over 40 years. He strapped himself into the giant Qantas jumbo at Heathrow for his first ever flight with all the enthusiasm of a boy on his first trip to the seaside. His spirit of adventure was rekindled and he once again amazed the Australians with that same chirpiness and courage he had shown in Brisbane, when he rose from his hospital bed with a high temperature to play a remarkable innings of 83 in the Queensland heat. Now, 45 years on, he was probably the only one of us who could have induced an Australian barman to put a can of ice-cold beer under the hot tap before pouring it.

Nestling under the Lofty mountains there can be few more picturesque settings than the Adelaide Oval, or indeed many better batting wickets. The uncertainty of conditions in Brisbane compared drastically with the generally accepted pace of the Perth wickets, though possibly our experience in West Australia was an exception. Our pace attack in 1958 looked pretty formidable. Tyson, Trueman, Statham, Loader with Bailey in support would on the face of it have a field day on the lightning fast Perth pitches. To their complete chagrin the middle was flooded (by hand) a couple of days before our first game and as Tyson roared in downwind the ball barely reached stump height. Strange how these sets of circumstances appear all round the world!

In my playing days one felt a real patriotic bond between England and New Zealand. The heroism of the New Zealand troops during the war was still very much in many people's minds as I set sail in September 1951 on the *SS Rangitata* to undertake a five-months coaching appointment in Auckland. A voyage of some five weeks with stops only at Panama and off the shores of Fletcher Christian's Pitcairn Island, was an unforgettable experience. Apart from a few English immigrants the passenger list was almost exclusively one of middle-aged Kiwis homeward bound after a visit to the Old Country. For many it had been the realisation of a lifetime's dream and something for which they had saved diligently for years previously. England still meant a great deal to them, and now it was their turn to show a great warmth of welcome and overwhelming hospitality to the likes of myself and my wife, on a first visit from a country which they had taken to their hearts. There was a great deal to recommend the leisurely shipboard life prior to the days of jet travel and one felt really fit and refreshed on arrival in Wellington.

A fine New Zealand side of 1949 had been decimated with the retirement of Hadlee, Donnelly, Scott, Wallace, Cowie and Burtt, and it was impossible to replace players of this calibre from the small cricketing population of the two islands. Rugby football has always been the principal love of the Kiwis and wherever one travelled, even throughout their summer, there was a crowd of youngsters to be seen punting the oval ball around. Many talented young cricketers were lost to the game due to the predominance of rugby. A prime example was that great All Black, Don Clarke, who I am sure, would have made a notable fast bowler.

Perhaps the best summing-up of life in New Zealand came from one-time Controller of BBC 1, Bryan Cowgill, when he said 'New Zealand – it closes every Friday'. The weekend, certainly in those days, meant a couple of days sailing or fishing or indeed moving down to a seaside cottage and family picnics on one of the many delightful coves or beaches. Yet even in midweek, Queens Street in Auckland was more than likely to be semi-deserted by 9.30 pm. I was fortunate enough to be allowed to play for Auckland in their Plunket Shield competition which entailed a trip to the South Island to play at Christchurch and Dunedin. The season, in fact, finished all too soon for me yet the memories of a marvellous week's holiday in Rotorua and the friendships which have lasted through to this day make me feel so sorry that I have never been able to return there. We left Auckland Harbour in great style aboard a Teal Flying Boat and hours later made an equally memorable splash down in Rose Bay, Sydney. Our journey home was completed on the *SS Stratheden* via the Suez Canal. Our round the world trip was surely one which must be the envy of all our modern jet-styled and highly paid international cricketers.

Whichever way you look at it there are bound to be lasting memories of a trip to India and Pakistan. I was never selected by MCC for this particular tour but thankfully George Duckworth, who assembled a Commonwealth side to go there, thought more of my talents than R.W.V. Robins and Co. Our trip to India coincided with Freddie Brown's MCC tour of Australasia in 1950-51 when, to put it mildly, I was more than puzzled by my omission. Brian Close, selected as the off spinner, had taken 20 wickets that summer which included seven for Yorkshire. I felt that my 166 wickets at 15 apiece might just have given me the edge, but the selectors in their wisdom had decided that my type of bowling was unlikely ever to present any problems to Australians! It all meant that I was particularly pleased to collect the compensation of a trip to India.

We left Tilbury the day after the England team but overhauled them in the Mediterranean and were tied up in Aden before they arrived. Come to think of it we would have surpassed them on the field as well, for this Commonwealth side was just about the best cricket team I ever played with. Les Ames was virtually a non-

Hobbs and Sutcliffe, the most successful opening partnership in Test match history. A great stand by them produced one of my favourite examples of the barracking from the Sydney Hill.

playing captain and Frank Worrell invariably did the job. In the batting order he followed three of the finest stroke players in England in Harold Gimblett, Laurie Fishlock and George Emmett. The Lancashire duo of Ken Grieves and John Ikin made the middle order. If there has been a more formidable quartet of spinners than Bruce Dooland, George Tribe, Sonny Ramadhin and myself in any touring party then I have not seen it. With Les Jackson, Derek Shackleton, Fred Ridgeway and Frank himself supplying pace and seam, it is small wonder we were undefeated in 27 tour matches.

George Duckworth was simply marvellous. He was a one-man management committee and he not only planned the whole tour but managed it single-handed, looking after the finances, the baggage and playing problems. He even found time to write a daily column. Remember too that the tour quickly followed partition between India and Pakistan. There were no five-star hotels, there was prohibition in Bombay province, and most of the accommodation was simple to say the least. Conditions, in fact, for a tour to India were generally very poor.

Below right: Boxing Day at Melbourne, 1974 and 77,000 watching Australia play England. I did not enjoy my matches at Melbourne as much as those at Sydney and elsewhere.

In Northern India, Patiala, the home of the Sikhs, produced the finest batting surface I ever saw. We were staggered to see an elephant between the shafts of the heavy roller. It was only a three-day match and scoring a rapid 435 for 7 we managed to win by an innings. Patiala's second innings featured an incident as humorous as I ever witnessed on a cricket field. It concerned George Tribe, our Australian left-arm wrist spinner, who was bowling wonderfully well but was having little luck and certainly none at all as far as the umpire was concerned. He had rapped various batsmen on the pads, shrieked his appeals and in return had received a bland Eastern smile and a shake of the head. The final batsman to be totally confused by George's mixture of chinamen and googlies was no less a person than the Maharajah of Patiala himself. A wonderful figure of a man and no mean performer with the bat, he still found himself in a tangle trying to cope with the brilliance of Tribe. Twice he was beaten on the back foot and twice more the appeals rang out. I smiled to myself feeling certain that it was impossible that the Maharajah would be dispatched lbw. George, however, was unconvinced. Yet another appeal, more fervent than before, rang out and yet again the answer came back in the negative. At his wit's end the chunky Australian turned on the umpire, shook him hard by the shoulders and yelled at him 'Don't be such a bloody fool, have another look'. The trembling umpire, looking down at the giant-sized batsman, then again at the raging Tribe, took a deep breath, calmed himself and said 'My word, Mr Tribe, you are right. I am sorry, Sir, but you are out' and up went the dreaded finger. It is not a ploy I would recommend to our present day bowlers if Mr Harold Bird is officiating.

Putting a budding Bert Sutcliffe or John Reid into the right position while doing a bit of coaching in New Zealand.

Most people would take a lot of persuasion that my 19 wickets in a single Test against Australia was not my best-ever bowling performance. Statistically, of course, there can be few arguments yet I believe that the best spell of bowling in my career took place in the Bombay Test match on this Indian tour. By the second day the wicket had become a paradise for batsmen and despite a healthy first innings lead we were always going to struggle to dismiss the Indians a second time. The heat was unbearable and the humidity typical of Bombay as we took the field faced with an Indian batting line up in which the first eight places were filled by Merchant, Mushtaq Ali, Umrigar, Hazare, Phadkar, Adhikari, Mankad and Manjrekar. Despite a brilliant partnership of 225 between Umrigar (130) and Hazare (115) we finally managed to work our way through the side and knocked off the necessary runs for a ten-wicket victory. My analysis in that second innings read: 65 overs, 34 maidens, 88 runs, 5 wickets. I do not believe, taking everything into consideration, that I ever bowled better.

It is some time now since official England tours to South Africa

One of the best touring teams I was in, a Commonwealth side to India in 1950-51. Here we are in Bombay. *Left to right, back:* Alf Barlow, Fred Ridgway, Dick Spooner, John Ikin, Derek Shackleton, Les Jackson, myself, Ken Grieves, George Emmett, Sonny Ramadhin. *Front:* Bruce Dooland, George Tribe, George Duckworth (manager), Les Ames, Frank Worrell, Laurie Fishlock and Harold Grimblett.

have taken place and those cricketers whose careers have fallen during this barren period can count themselves distinctly unfortunate. My first glimpse of South Africa came early in the war when our troopship spent four days in Durban. Arriving from a blacked-out Britain, with food and clothes rationed, and every other kind of shortage, it was like reaching the Promised Land. That brief stay whetted my appetite, and I seized an early opportunity to take up a coaching appointment in Durban soon after the war.

My stay in Durban coincided with the visit of Lindsay Hassett's all-conquering Australian tourists, which added a great deal of interest to the winter. Several years later I returned for a major MCC tour under Peter May's captaincy but after that there was a lapse of 19 years before I spent another pleasant few days at the Cape. A long trip indeed to make for an after-dinner speech!

There can be no doubt that South African cricket had become a real power in world cricket when the embargo came down, though when we arrived in 1956 for Peter May's tour it had not then reached that general high all round standard. On reflection South

Africa had a highly talented squad of around 15 players but in many of the Provincial centres the standard dropped quite appreciably. Consequently during a five-month tour one faced tough opposition only in the five Test matches and in the fixtures with Transvaal and Natal, and one had ample opportunity to enjoy the hospitality which was showered endlessly upon us.

A major problem for our trio of pace bowlers was the altitude in Johannesburg, overcome to a certain extent by a ready supply of oxygen in the dressing room. Frank Tyson was a sufferer there in the Test match, where he was faced by a gritty performance from opener Jackie McGlew. Showing all the courage in the world the diminutive McGlew was getting right behind everything that speedster Tyson let loose. At the end of one particular fearsome over I passed Frank as we changed ends. 'Say what you like, Frank, but this little fellow has a ton of guts' I suggested. Frank gulped another lung full of air and quickly replied 'Yes, and next over we may well have a look at them'. Fast bowlers have not changed over the years.

By the time the tour ended I had in my two visits spent twelve months experiencing conditions in South Africa. Sufficient time to appreciate, possibly, a little more than many people back in England who had never set foot in South Africa and yet insisted on voicing opinions on Apartheid, that the problems were not always one-sided. At the same time I never felt entirely comfortable there, and was constantly appalled at the treatment of the Blacks, the Cape Coloureds and the Indians. It is certainly not a country I could emigrate to. When finally pressure by the Government on MCC saw us suspend international cricket with South Africa, it was a decision any fair-minded person had to agree with.

During the years that followed I had several opportunities to revisit South Africa but still felt that it would be wrong to do so until three years ago when an offer, quite out of the ordinary, came my way. This was an invitation by the *Cape Herald* newspaper to fly to Cape Town to present a trophy awarded to the Sportsman of the Year. The difference was that the *Cape Herald* looks after the interests of the Cape Coloureds and with one exception all the contestants would come from the coloured population. At least it would give me a first-class opportunity to see if conditions had changed after an absence of 18 years and, more important, to spend some time with the coloured population, which had never been possible during an official MCC tour.

It would be fair to say that my first impression on arrival in Cape Town was that some progress had been made towards multi-racial sport. I was certainly amused when the waiter at the hotel no longer asked me if I wanted my coffee 'black or white' but instead 'with or without'. However the cricket matches I saw, and which concerned only the Cape Coloureds, were still played under the most primitive

Coaching in South Africa. I bowl to Alan Oakman in Johannesburg while South African schoolboys watch how it's done.

of conditions which still differed greatly from the fine facilities that came the way of the white cricketers.

During these last three years since my visit I have been reliably informed that enormous strides have been made to ensure that competitors are now judged on merit and not on race and colour. In fact the South African Minister for Sport has gone on record as saying that now there is far less discrimination over there than in many other countries. More to the point, this view is shared by the genial president of the South African Cricket Union, Rached Varachia, a resident Indian of Johannesburg. He goes on to point out that South Africa have now complied with all the conditions laid down in 1962 by the International Cricket Council. With complete integration there is now one single controlling body, who select sides solely on merit. Additionally, seating on all grounds has become de-segregated and common facilities are now shared by Whites, Blacks and Coloureds alike. If the ICC delegation discover on their next visit to Johannesburg that these factors can be verified, then surely we shall look forward to welcoming South Africa back into the cricket field. It remains to be seen, however, what sort of

One of the best off-spinners I've seen, Hugh Tayfield gets Tony Lock caught by Jackie McGlew during MCC's tour of South Africa in 1956-57.

view our politicians take, for it is fairly obvious that in relation to integration the cricket authorities have moved far ahead of the Government. If the block against South Africa's return to international cricket remains, it would be the classic case of politics in cricket.

In spite of so many unforgettable experiences around Australia and New Zealand, India and South Africa, I think that possibly I cherish my visits to the West Indies most of all. In fairness I have spent more time in the Caribbean than anywhere else, and possibly a first overseas cricket tour has the greatest impact of all, particularly when it comes, as it did for me, after just a handful of first-class matches in 1947. I understand it was on the recommendation of umpire Frank Chester that I was added to the party already selected for the three and a half months tour of the West Indies under the captaincy of G.O. Allen. Naturally I was well versed with the performances and career records of all the members of the party, yet as individuals the majority were total strangers to me as we left on a cold December morning by train to Garston Docks in Liverpool.

What a transformation has taken place in the arrangements for overseas tours in the 30 years since 1948. The press photographs of Billy Griffith and 'Gubby' Allen setting forth in their light-coloured belted raincoats, with trilby hats pulled well down, made them look

Not the Mafia, but the MCC party departing for the West Indies on December 23, 1947. *From left:* S.C. Griffith, Godfrey Evans, Jack Robertson, Gubby Allen, myself, Maurice Tremlett and Gerald Smithson.

more like a modern version of the CIA. Who would think these days of sending England off on a Caribbean tour on board an empty banana boat of 4,000-odd tons, to be bounced around in mid-Atlantic gales for 14 days? Mind you, if they did, it would in all probability cost a shade more than the £25 per head paid by MCC. At the time of writing I read that our top players in Australia for the 1978-79 tour of similar length will be paid £8,500 which again is a slight improvement on the £300 we received. One also knows they were not faced with a batting line-up which includes players of the calibre of Stollmeyer, Headley, Weekes, Worrell and Walcott, to name just a few.

Let me emphasise that there is not the slightest trace of jealousy or envy in my pen. Delighted I am that our present day cricketers are being well rewarded financially, but in no way would I have foregone my tour to West Indies or exchanged it for the latest tour to take place 'down under'. I enjoyed playing my cricket when I did. Strangely very few cricketers complained about wage structures.

Left: Winston Place, Lancashire opening batsman, who recovered from some bad moments on the banana boat to the West Indies to share some good times when we got there.

Above: Palm trees make the Barbados ground picturesque. My first experience of cricket in the West Indies was on this ground two days after a choppy crossing.

There are so many indefinables to playing cricket round the world which can never be translated directly into pounds and pence. Time has proved that the Huttons, the Comptons, the Washbrooks, the Bedsers, the Baileys etc have no real worries where the next fiver is coming from.

One person however on that tour did have a problem or two on board the SS *Tetela*. Dear Winston Place, the Lancashire opener, was not a good sailor. He took to his cabin before we left Merseyside and two days out, on Christmas Day, with fierce gales restricting our speed to eight knots, it did not look as though Winston would ever survive to take guard again. By Boxing Day he was meekly offering anyone £50 to shoot him!

Finally we limped into Barbados two days late, and due to play our first game against the all-conquering Barbados XI two days later. A new generation of cricketers had emerged in the West Indies over the war years, and of course many of our side were unknown as well, and with this in mind a party was quickly arranged to give us the opportunity of informal introduction. The first of these superb players I met was the giant Clyde Walcott and after chatting most affably with him for some time I moved away and introduced myself to a rather more staid and elderly gentleman, quietly sipping his rum and ginger all alone. It transpired that he was the umpire who would officiate not only in the Colony match

93

but also in the Tests. This was a stroke of luck. Quickly I found a waiter and secured a steady supply of rum cocktails, and no question my newly found friend really began to mellow. All the time I could see Clyde eyeing me with a good deal of suspicion. Finally I moved back to him and he said 'You do know who that is?' Triumphantly I replied 'Yes, of course, he told me he is the Test match umpire' and with a sly dig added 'and after this little session, I'd keep my legs out of the way if I were you'. Walcott's previous serious expression changed rapidly and he broke into a giant-sized grin. 'If I were you I would go back and get him another drink – he is my uncle!' Records will prove that umpire Walcott stood in that series and I

Frank Worrell was the most elegant of the three 'Ws' and certainly played me with more comfort than did Weekes and Walcott.

cannot remember a single appeal for lbw being upheld in my favour. For all that we remained firm friends for many years.

Arguments still rage around the three 'Ws'. Was Frank Worrell, Everton Weekes or Clyde Walcott the best of all? Possibly there were occasions when all three could lay claim to that distinction. Frank certainly played me with more authority than his two colleagues, yet on occasions both Clyde and Everton took far heavier toll than the elegant Worrell. If I was not bowling, Everton Weeks was the one I really enjoyed watching, and in my view he was overall the best. For years I was struck by the originality of his Christian name. Of course he was not alone in this respect – consider Rohan Babucal

95

Kanhai, Garfield St. Aubrun Sobers or even Frank Maglinne Worrell. After thinking about it for some time I asked Everton where his name originated from. He certainly seemed serious enough when he told me that his father was a great supporter of English soccer, and in fact Everton was his favourite side. I could not help suggesting to him that it was just as well that the old man did not support West Bromwich Albion!

With so many of our leading players discovering acceptable excuses for turning down the 1947 tour our side was never good enough to contain the brilliant West Indians, yet for me there were a host of lingering memories. Billy Griffith's epic Trinidad century was one, another the sheer guts of 'Gubby' Allen undertaking a tour of the West Indies as a pace bowler at the age of 45. I learned a good deal from some wonderful bowling spells by Dick Howarth, who never lost his sense of humour.

By no means least was a car journey from Montego Bay to Port Antonio, to catch the boat home, made in the company of Ken Cranston and Joe Hardstaff. Under normal circumstances an hour and a half would see the trip completed, but our running time that day was close on seven hours. Ken and Joe were saying farewell to the West Indians for ever and insisted on sampling the product at every rum shop on the way. I cannot recall who footed the bill, but dear Joe had finished his tour allowance a good six weeks previously.

Seven years later I returned to the Caribbean with MCC captained by Len Hutton under vastly different circumstances and this time with a full strength England side. Our batting line up in the Trinidad Test was Hutton, Bailey, May, Compton, Watson, Graveney and to bowl we had Trueman, Statham, Bailey, Lock and myself. For all that the West Indies made 681 for 8 and the contribution of the three 'Ws' was 497. Our five front line bowlers took five of those wickets at a cost of 598! With the follow-on at 150 we needed 532 to save it, and thanks to May, Compton and Graveney we just about made it. In fact after a couple of days in the field in exceptionally hot weather the West Indies were looking most jaded as I was joined in the middle by Fred Trueman, as the second or possibly the third new ball was due. The one exception appeared to be Frank King, the Barbados fast bowler, who was still as lively as ever and letting loose his fair share of bouncers. To take the new ball with him was Frank Worrell, and by this time Frank was hardly medium pace. Fred called a mid-wicket conference. So many people have asked me what batsmen talk about when they have their periodic chats in the middle. This particular conversation I recall vividly, despite taking no part in it myself. It was a Trueman monologue which went something like this 'Have assessed the situation, Jim lad – thee take King and I'll look after Worrell'.

Cricketer and tennis player enjoying a round of golf. Fred Perry and I going round the easy way in Jamaica.

One might have thought Barry Knight, Trevor Bailey and I could have found another game in Jamaica in 1964.

Blindly and dumbly I agreed, and minutes later, in attempting something quite out of my province, namely a hook shot from a King bouncer, I was zig-zagging my way to the pavilion with an eye pouring blood and requiring more stitches than I can remember. The last words I recall came naturally from Fred: 'That's the shrewdest assessment I've made for some time.'

Since those early visits to the West Indies there have been several ugly and unhappy cricketing moments in Jamaica, Trinidad and Guyana. I suppose that it all goes to prove that we were not far wrong back in 1947 when the unanimous decision was that Barbados held pride of place for visiting English sides. With the development of the St James coast and the subsequent luxury hotels, the island has become a regular winter rendezvous for the big names in the world of sport and entertainment. Very obviously there have been changes down at Kensington Oval, with a big new stand aptly christened 'the three Ws'. The wickets there also no longer present bowlers with little or no hope. The great enthusiasm for the game remains. A continuous supply of natural cricketers continues to flow from this island which in size is no larger than the Isle of Wight. To have begun my Test career on this ground 31 years ago was a great thrill, and even now I look forward to my visits to the island with the same anticipation and youthful enthusiasm that I did so many years ago as a player.

League Cricket

Throughout my long association with Surrey County Cricket Club I cherished an ambition: that when my first-class career was over I would return whence I started and play one season in league cricket as a professional. For years I had looked back with affection on those early days when as a schoolboy I had played for Saltaire in the Bradford League. I relished the keen competition of those days and the dramas which unfolded with each successive Saturday afternoon. Before I ever made my first team debut at the age of 16 I knew by heart the names and performances of Spen Victoria's opening pair down to Windhill's two fast bowlers. My one particular hero was the Baildon Green professional, George Senior, a balding opening batsman who hailed from Huddersfield. George used to pack the crowds in at Jenny Lane. He was no respecter of persons or reputations, and as a 12-year-old I watched him destroy the West Indian professionals, Martindale and St Hill with a series of hooks and drives out of the Compton book. By a strange quirk of circumstance my first over in Bradford League cricket was bowled at George whose score stood at 46. He cracked my first ball for four, gave the collectors time to take the boxes round the ground and then played outside a straight half volley. He gave me a sly wink, a pat on the back, and was gone. I never saw him again for over 30 years until he arrived at Headingley a few years back. He was then 70 years old, as sprightly as ever, and had just retired as a Huddersfield League umpire. The half hour I spent with him that day meant more to me than dinner with the great Sir Donald Bradman. When I chided him for not contacting me earlier, he said he was too shy and doubted if I would remember him!

I played my last season in the Bradford League in 1940 just prior to embarking overseas and that was for me a memorable year. With each league side allowed four professionals, and County cricket suspended, there arrived each weekend a great influx of first-class cricketers. My own club had an affiliation it seemed with Derbyshire; consequently Bill Copson, George and Alf Pope and Les Townsend took the field in Roberts Park. Charlie Harris and Walter Keeton opened for Bingley and further along the road Eddie Paynter and Winston Place would set the Keighley innings on its way. At neighbouring Windhill, Learie Constantine, Les Ames and

George Dawkes bolstered the locals and so it went on. Little wonder that bowling no more than medium pace my few wickets cost me 30 runs apiece, though I managed a few runs and even ran into three figures at Bankfoot.

Little did I realise then that from those wonderful days right through to the present time I should never see another Bradford League game. Vivid memories stayed with me over the years. Though League cricket had been so much a part of my life as a boy, would I really enjoy it if I returned as a Test match cricketer? I really wanted to get it all into perspective once more, and that is why I was determined to play a full season in 1960. When my retirement was announced in the national Press, there was no shortage of offers forthcoming, though not a whisper from the Bradford League. Times, of course, had changed, and no league side in Yorkshire could compete with the fees being offered in Lancashire, Staffordshire and Birmingham. To accept an engagement in Lancashire involved spending the whole summer in the North and that was quite impracticable. I was on the point of signing for an eminent Birmingham League side when I discovered that playing as 'amateurs' in the same team were several ex-Warwickshire players. Not surprising that the terms offered to me were far from generous – and I would be the clown paying tax.

Suddenly out of the blue came an offer from Norton, who played in the North Staffordshire League, and their chairman Tom Talbot came down to see me. Tom, a wealthy Midland industrialist, was typical of many who devote themselves to both soccer and cricket in that area. He was also a director of Port Vale and responsible for persuading Eddie Baily to leave that great Tottenham side of the 1950s and move up to play in the Potteries.

In fact I rang Eddie prior to signing for Norton, and he said that he hoped I would settle in quicker than he did. Recalling his days with Spurs, the masters of the push and run game, he told me of his first experience in the Potteries. The centre forward touched the ball to him, Eddie slipped it back to the centre half who gave it an almighty belt into the visitors' penalty area. The opposition full back returned it first time in similar manner and the active bombardment went on for another 10 minutes. Eddie, mesmerised, was rooted to the centre circle, his head turning left and right like a Wimbledon spectator. He hardly had another touch throughout the first half. 'You will find it very different' he said.

Still, I was perfectly satisfied with my contract with Tom Talbot and I was to receive £60 a match (most of it paid out of Tom's pocket) for 20 Saturday afternoon matches and two Bank Holiday fixtures. In addition there would be collections for five wickets with the ball and 50 runs with the bat. I also remembered that just a year earlier the fee for a five-day Test match was £75 – and that meant foregoing the match fees for two Surrey County games. One hundred thousand people would watch a Test match yet we should be lucky to get a couple of thousand at Norton.

The ground was a very pleasant one; neat, tidy and very well kept. It really had become Tom Talbot's baby. His ambitions knew no limit. He was desperate for success and travelled the country for the big name professional. The previous year had seen Frank Worrell performing wonders as his professional and when I told him I should only be available for one season, he quickly began to negotiate for a replacement. No less a person than Gary Sobers followed me to Norton. As a Saturday afternoon cricketer I could not hope to emulate the feats of our two West Indian cricketing knights, though it would be fair to say that I had a successful season.

Each Saturday morning I would leave London around 9 am and drive up on the recently opened M1 in time to reach Stoke around midday. As the matches did not end until around 7.30 or 8 pm I stayed on with the boys and returned home early on Sunday morning. This routine I followed on my first appearance as professional for Norton at the end of April 1960 when the visitors were Crewe. Tom met me in Hanley and took me along to the ground where I first met my skipper Jim Flannery. Jim, a schoolmaster by profession, turned out to have a good cricket brain, was a useful middle-order batsman, a fearless close fielder and a great help to me.

In the dressing room my new colleagues drifted in and were slowly revealed to me. What a cross section of Staffordshire life they represented. The first arrival was the local policeman and thank goodness I only received a single 'hullo' as he hung up his helmet. Not surprisingly he looked me up and down. Prior to my signing he was the team's off break bowler, but as he was also a useful batsman his place was never in jeopardy. Following closely behind came, believe it or not, the village blacksmith, a job inherited from father and grandfather. Stocky and powerfully built, he hit the ball with tremendous strength and I vividly recall him square cutting a quickish bowler for six in that first game. If that surprised me then I was dumbfounded when I saw him come on to bowl – surely no other blacksmith had ever bowled slow left-arm wrist spinners. In sharp contrast came Dave Wilson, an excellent pace bowler who had experience with the Kent second eleven and was now at Keele University.

Announcing his arrival with a couple of resounding belches and a quick dash to the 'loo' came Steve, who proved to be a roundish arm slinger and on his day likely to pick up valuable wickets. It also transpired he was not always welcome at the local dance halls on

Dennis Cox, (*left*), changed his style with Crewe, and became a new and highly successful league cricketer. Alec Bedser seems to be protecting him from ribbing from Oval colleagues Surridge, McIntyre, Eric Bedser and myself.

Saturday night. I must say I found him a most genuine character and certainly had plenty of laughs with him over the season. On one occasion half way through the season I was trying hard to tempt a young player to try to hit me out of the ground. I had pushed two or three balls through quickly and then held the next one back and dropped it fractionally shorter. The young lad took the bait and skied it into the outfield where Steve had been perfectly positioned to take the catch. To my utter chagrin there was no sign of Steve. The lunch-time pints had caught up with him and in desperation he had leapt over the adjacent brick wall to relieve himself. Throw in a draughtsman, a ledger clerk, and a young sixth-former, and we had the nucleus of what, I suppose, is fairly typical of any league side. We were a collection of very different characters, but hardly had a word of friction throughout the year.

We were away to a good start with a seven-wicket victory over Crewe. By sheer coincidence Crewe's new professional was my old friend and colleague from the Oval, Dennis Cox. Dennis had arrived after a successful spell with Walsall in the Birmingham League which had brought him a much improved contract with Crewe, and he was really keen to prove his worth. He was destined for a few early shocks. I managed to pick up five cheap wickets as we dismissed Crewe for around 70, but Dennis's fast-medium seamers created no problems as we raced to an easy win.

Through the medium of the local papers I followed Dennis's fortunes over the next three weeks and was saddened to see that he was finding no kind of form at all. Then suddenly he hit the local headlines with 20 wickets in the space of three games. I was genuinely pleased for him, but flabbergasted when he explained his change of fortune. Apparently he decided that he was getting nowhere at all bowling in his medium-paced style and decided overnight completely to change his method. He took three or four strides to the wicket and bowled his own version of slow leg spinners or to be more precise leg rollers. Finding sufficient accuracy and enough turn from the pitch to confuse the best players he went on from strength to strength. With his powerful hitting he turned out to be as good a professional as any in the league, and Crewe were delighted to give him a long term contract.

For my part I was picking up a steady haul of wickets but precious few runs at number six in the order. It had been many years since I had concentrated with the bat and trying to do so now I found myself in such a defensive frame of mind that a good half hour in the middle had hardly brought a run. Time is at a premium in Saturday afternoon cricket and I cannot recall reaching double figures in the first half-dozen matches. A change of thinking was called for and it coincided with our visit to Bignall End. This was the club with a long association with the Ikin family. John began playing there as a

Another league metamorphosis Cliff Gladwin, who once won a Test match with a leg-bye batting number eleven, was an aggressive opening bat with Longton.

schoolboy, and when he completed a distinguished first-class career he came back to the village and continued to enjoy his cricket.

Nowhere in the world have I ever met a more respected cricketer than John. He has given back to the game far more than he ever received from it. Alongside him on that day was a young teenage wicket-keeper, Bob Taylor, who caught my eye. In my book he has had few peers behind the stumps in recent years and only the extra batting ability of Alan Knott had prevented him from winning a regular England position.

For the first time at Bignall End we found a wet and responsive pitch and my 7 for 20 saw us dismiss the home side for 95. It was obvious that we should also struggle for runs, so I suggested to Jim Flannery that I should move up to number three and try my luck playing a few shots. A wicket fell in the very first over, so putting caution aside, I tried my plan and I began to throw the bat about. The ploy paid off, and I scored fifty in even time as we took the points with a nine-wicket victory. This set my pattern for the future, and adopting similar tactics I hammered a 70 against Stone and a further 60-odd in the return match at Crewe. Cliff Gladwin, who was Longton's professional, went even further. He opened the batting and was totally unrecognisable as the doughty defensive tail-ender with Derbyshire. He let the bat fly at anything pitched up 'in his half' and it paid handsome dividends. One must remember too that league grounds are quite small by comparison with county grounds and standards of fielding and catching fall well short of those of first-class cricket.

Talking of wet pitches brings to memory our visit to the lovely ground of Ashcombe Park, where my old friend and adversary, Sonny Ramadhin, was the resident professional. There have been few more successful league bowlers than Sonny, who for years had left a trail of destruction behind him wherever he had been employed. I looked forward to renewing our encounter. Bowling was Ashcombe Park's strength, for in addition to the redoubtable 'Ram' they possessed a very quick and lively left-arm over-the-wicket bowler. There had been no rain in Staffordshire for a couple of weeks prior to our game and a good crowd were settling under the trees as I walked out to have a look at the pitch. At one end it was rock hard with plenty of grass, yet at the other end it was easily possible to push your thumb a good half inch into the turf. I turned round to see Sonny close behind me with a great grin on his face. 'You have not been here before, have you' he said. 'You know it is the only ground I know where it rains at one end'. I had a feeling there may have been one or two more like it in the distant parts of Lancashire. Still, who was I to complain. We did in fact have a cracking good game and only by the narrowest of margins did we come off second best.

From the day I first met him, Sonny Ramadhin has never failed to intrigue me, and despite the ups and downs of his career he stands very high in my esteem. The original country boy from southern Trinidad, he was scarcely known in West Indies cricket prior to his sensational tour of England in 1950. During those early days he was the constant shadow of his mentor, Frank Worrell, and hardly ever strayed from his side. He saw his first train at Paddington Station, he gazed in disbelief at a Joe Davis snooker century and he must have thought the world had come to a grinding halt when encountering a Hyde Park corner traffic jam. None of this had the slightest effect on him once John Goddard put the ball in his hand. He began to mesmerise the greatest of English batsmen – I doubt whether two or three at the most had the slightest idea which way the ball would turn. In the Manchester Test match I watched from 22 yards as the great Len Hutton found himself in all kinds of trouble, and I am just as positive that Denis Compton was no wiser.

He reigned supreme over English batsmen until his second tour and the Birmingham Test of 1957. It seemed we had no answer to him once again as he demolished us with 7 for 49 in the first innings. Then came Peter May with the greatest innings of his career, a brilliant undefeated 285 and a world record partnership with Colin Cowdrey (154) of 411. No one could ever possibly detract from this

Sonny Ramadhin, to my mind one of the best and certainly one of the most intriguing slow bowlers. Ashcombe Park, where he was professional, was an intriguing pitch, where it appeared to rain only at one end.

performance, but my heart bled for little 'Ram'. Colin, when in doubt, pushed out the left pad hour after hour and Ramadhin swears to this day that he was lbw on no less than 30 occasions. So Colin survived to grow in confidence. Ramadhin was mastered but never collared. His second innings figures were 98 overs, 35 maidens, 179 runs and 2 wickets. There is no doubt this marathon feat took its toll, and by the end of the series Sonny's last seven wickets cost him 498 runs.

He was ideally suited to English conditions, not only because of our more responsive pitches but even more so, I am sure, because of our problems of light coupled with the background difficulties on many grounds. A quick arm action, a black hand, the absence of good sight screens and a shortage of sunshine and blue skies made life difficult for English batsmen. He never posed the same threats in Australia, India or West Indies. I played against him many times in 1950, and in common with others I could never pick which ball was an off break and which a leg break. The following winter I toured India with Sonny in a Commonwealth side and he bowled at me on our arrival in the nets at Bombay. It was a different story, and almost immediately I could spot quite clearly the difference between the off spinner and the leg break. Once this was implanted in my mind it remained there for good. Even years later at Ashcombe Park I spotted the difference – not that it did me a great deal of good for whether you could read him or not Ramadhin remained in the highest class and continued to be a prolific wicket taker.

No mention of Staffordshire cricket would be complete without reference to the Maestro himself – Sydney F. Barnes. The first time the magic name ever penetrated my young ears coincided with my first meeting with a very great Yorkshireman, George Herbert Hirst, who back in 1906 became the only man to score 2,000 runs and take 200 wickets in a season. I listened open-mouthed in wonderment to a conversation he had with Herbert Sutcliffe. They did not always agree with each other, but Herbert nodded his head approvingly when George Hirst pronounced that 'Sydney Barnes was the greatest bowler there has ever been and what's more the greatest bowler there ever will be'.

That was 40 years ago and nothing I have heard or read since has suggested that their judgement was far out. I saw Barnes play only once – guesting as a professional against Saltaire when he must have been well into his sixties! His control was remarkable and if the nip and turn had lost something with the passing of the years, he still collected his five wickets. Years later I spoke to him at length one day at Lord's and tried to discover the secret of his amazing performances. Never before or since have I met anybody with so much genuine confidence in his own ability. So much so that he said

Nobody can play long in Staffordshire League cricket without being told of the exploits of Syd Barnes by one old-timer or another. He would have many supporters for the 'greatest bowler ever' title.

it was nothing unusual for him to bowl an inswinger, a fast off break and a leg cutter in the same over, and even on odd occasions to slip in a googly. All this with the greatest accuracy and control. 'Keep trying something different' he said to me. It is incredible to remember that this variety of attack was combined with a pace something akin to that of Alec Bedser. As we shook hands I instantly knew that he had something else in common with the 'Big Fellow' – it was more than a touch of arthritis that gave those enormous fingers a gnarled and knotty appearance.

I have no complaint that I was never allowed to forget the name of Sydney Barnes during my enjoyable year in Staffordshire cricket. Barely a Saturday went by without a reminder of him coming my way usually, of course, from the more elderly members. Once, after what I thought was a luckless day at Porthill Park when my three wickets had not been cheap ones by any means, I was surrounded in the pavilion by what must have been the last remnants of the Barnes Fan Club. They looked me up and down in turn before the most senior of the trio promptly downgraded me with the remark that they had all seen S.F. take 8 for 3 on that very pitch!

All too soon the season came to an end and I was sorry when I finally said goodbye. Everyone had been most kind and helpful. Prior to my departure I gave a small party in Hanley for the players, wives and officials. Some people wondered why I should want to do this, but cricket remains very much a team game and even the highest paid professional (particularly a bowler) is dependent on those around him.

I had done what I set to do and had seen league cricket once again at first hand. I have never taken my opponents lightly, no matter what the conditions may have been. The folly of doing so has never been more forcibly demonstrated to me, albeit in a jocular manner, than the following season when I turned out for Essex at Worcester over a weekend. Jack Flavell had a benefit game at Halesowen on the Sunday and along with one or two Essex boys I went along to play for him. It was a lovely day and a big crowd turned up. After half an hour or so Jack tossed me the ball and off a couple of paces I bowled to a very determined character at the far end. A plain dark blue cap pulled well over his eyes, he came doggedly forward, bat and pad close together and killed the spin stone dead each ball of the over. I proceeded for the next four overs to toss the ball higher and higher but each time I received precisely the same treatment. I really felt the big crowd were becoming somewhat restless and after five maidens I said to the lad 'You know there is a lot of people here wanting some action; don't you think you should play a shot or two – this is like playing in a Test Match'. Quick as a flash came the response 'Aye that's right about a Test Match – the only difference is that you are not getting any wickets.'

From Capricorn to Saggitarius

Two of the best off spin bowlers I was privileged to play against were both South Africans, namely Athol Rowan and Hugh Tayfield. Some time ago when browsing through Wisden I discovered that Hugh was born on 30 January and Athol on 7 February. My own birthday falls on 9 February which makes all three of us born under the sign of Aquarius. A little further research quickly brought to light the names of Fred Trueman, Andy Roberts and Michael Holding (what a trio of pace bowlers) who are also Aquarians, together with two highly skilled medium pacers in Neil Hawke and Fazal Mahmoud. In direct contrast Test batsmen born under this sign were very hard to come by – I could discover only one living Englishman, John Hampshire of Yorkshire, with a mere eight caps. Australia could provide three world class batsmen in Bobby Simpson, Bill Lawry and Norman O'Neill, but for all that it seemed to me that if a couple of doting cricket fanatics wished to produce an England batsman of the future, they would be well advised to make sure the birth did not fall between 21 January and 19 February.

If on the other hand they ignited the spark a month earlier a vastly different story would be the case. The sign of Capricorn has produced such brilliant batsmen as Arthur Morris and Bruce Mitchell as openers followed in any order you like by Peter May, Rohan Kanhai, Colin Cowdrey, Clyde Walcott, the Nawab of Pataudi and Johnny Waite. Yet very few babies born over the Christmas holiday period became Test match bowlers. Wayne Daniel is the only pace bowler on my list, with Johnny Wardle and Clarrie Grimmett to look after the spin department. The two months period from 21 March to 21 May, covering Aries and Taurus, threw up only one fast bowler, Ernie McCormick, yet Gemini, following next, saw the birth of those two magnificent Lancastrians Tyson and Statham, with Davidson in support.

So what does it all mean? Judging by the coverage given in almost every newspaper and magazine, in every country, there must be a vast following for 'what the stars foretell'. Mind you only a small percentage of readers will ever admit to being influenced by what is apparently in store for them. One who did read avidly through the Sundays each week was that wonderful character Sagittarian Charlie Harris of Notts. It is said that if he were told that his lucky number for the week was 16, he would go into bat on Monday morning, play quietly at the first 15 balls he received and take an almighty crack at the next one.

I myself believe these forecasts have no value whatsoever. But it is not easy to discard the evidence of the years.

For instance, the Arian type is active, energetic and muscular. The movements are quick and impulsive and the whole personality is intensely alive. Of my eleven, Bill Edrich, Alan Knott, Joe Hardstaff and Cliff Gladwin are surely typical.

The Libran type is one whose strength lies in his powers of concentration, his intensity of application and his capacity for sustained effort. This is followed by short periods of complete relaxation, during which he usually declines to use any of his faculties. Is it coincidence that Geoffrey Boycott, Bill Ponsford, Richie Benaud and Ray Lindwall all fall into this group?

With these thoughts in mind it seemed it might be fun, and I emphasize the word fun, to select 12 sides to correspond with their star signs, attempting of course to mould each eleven into something like an all-round combination but to restrict the selection at the time of writing only to living cricketers. The following were the results.

Rohan Kanhai (*left*) and Peter May (*right*) are just two more batsmen born under the favourable batting influence of Capricorn. May is being caught by Charlie Harris, who used to base his batting on what the stars foretold.

Capricorn

22 December to
20 January

Harmonious signs
Taurus, Virgo, Libra

The Capricorn character takes life earnestly and is generally an upholder of tradition and authority. This must certainly apply to the majority of this side.

MORRIS, A.R. Australia
MITCHELL, B. South Africa
*MAY, P.B.H. England
KANHAI, R.B. West Indies
COWDREY, M.C. England
WALCOTT, C.L. West Indies
PATAUDI, Nawab of. India
†WAITE, J.H.B. South Africa
WARDLE, J.H. England
DANIEL, W.W. West Indies
GRIMMETT, C.V. Australia

The Capricorn side has a wealth of batsmen but an obvious shortage of pace or even medium paced bowling, so much so that Clyde Walcott would be required to use the new ball with Wayne Daniel. At least spinners Johnny Wardle and Clarrie Grimmett should have stacks of runs to play with.

Above: Colin Cowdrey, one of many brilliant batsmen born under Capricorn.
Left: Clyde Walcott, another Capricorn batsman.
Opposite: Aquarius is rich in fast bowlers (and off-break bowlers!) and Andy Roberts would open the attack.
Opposite below: Bobby Simpson would get the Aquarius batting off to a sound start.

Aquarius

21 January to
19 February
Harmonious signs
Libra, Gemini, Aries

The Aquarian is not in awe of tradition or authority. He will never refrain from turning on those in higher office, particularly when in search for the truth. Could there possibly be a rebel or two amongst my Aquarian team?

*SIMPSON, R.B. Australia
LAWRY, W.M. Australia
CONGDON, B.E. New Zealand
O'NEILL, N.C. Australia
HAMPSHIRE, J.H. England
†TALLON, D. Australia
HAWKE, N.J.N. Australia
TAYFIELD, H.J. South Africa
LAKER, J.C. England
TRUEMAN, F.S. England
ROBERTS, A.M.E. West Indies

There is no shortage of Aquarian bowlers, particularly when one considers that Athol Rowan, Michael Holding and Fazal Mahmoud are not included. The middle order is perhaps a little thin leaving one to regret that Patsy Hendren was not born thirty years later.

Pisces

20 February to
20 March

Harmonious signs
Cancer, Scorpio, Virgo

STOLLMEYER, J.B. West Indies
McGLEW, D.J. South Africa
SIMPSON, R.T. England
WEEKES, E.D. West Indies
RICHARDS, I.V.A. West Indies
POLLOCK, R.G. South Africa
HAZARE, V.S. India
*CLOSE, D.B. England
†ENGINEER, F.M. India
JOHNSTONE, W.A. Australia
ADCOCK, N.A.T. South Africa

The Piscean, it is said, seldom succeeds in making money and rarely accumulates it. These are traits which I am pretty sure several of this team would wholly agree with.

The Pisces side is another immensely powerful batting combination. Pity any attack having to face Everton Weekes, Viv Richards and Graham Pollock after disposing of the first three. With no quality spin bowler in sight, Pisces would wish to avoid a dusty pitch.

Above: Farokh Engineer would keep wicket for Pisces.
Left: Pisces is powerful in batting, and Viv Richards goes in at five, followed by Graeme Pollock.
Opposite above: Aries is not the strongest of these sides, but at least there was never a better fighter than Bill Edrich.
Opposite, below: Wicket-keeping is no problem for Aries. Alan Knott looks after that department.

Aries

21 March to
20 April

Harmonious signs
Sagittarius, Leo

It is generally believed that Arians are known for their captaincy and leadership, but this does not apply to the game of cricket, judging by my team here.

AMISS, D.L. England
EDRICH, W.J. England
*WADEKAR, A.L. India
HARDSTAFF, J. England
KALLICHARAN, A.I. West Indies
UMRIGAR, P.R. India
BLAND, K.C. South Africa
LOXTON, S.J.E. Australia
†KNOTT, A.P.E. England
GLADWIN, C. England
COWIE, J. New Zealand

On paper the Aries side looks to be one of the weakest and strangely Australia provides only one player, Sam Loxton, who made only twelve international appearances. Clearly Aries is not a month for producing Australian Test cricketers. The late great S.F. Barnes would have put them in with a better chance.

Taurus

21 April to
21 May

Harmonious signs
Capricorn, Virgo,
Cancer

HUNTE, C.C. West Indies
FINGLETON, J.H. Australia
REDPATH, I.R. Australia
*DEXTER, E.R. England
WYATT, R.E.S. England
BURGE, P.J. Australia
WATKINS, A.J. England
†MURRAY, D.L. West Indies
McCORMICK, E.L. Australia
RAMADHIN, S. West Indies
VALENTINE, A.L. West Indies

The chief characteristic
of the Taurean is his
stability of character and
purpose. Steadfast in
mind, unshaken in
adversity and quietly
persistent in the face of
difficulties – like our two
opening bats?

A solid looking side is Taurus, with
the presence of the West Indian
spin twins denying a place to
Chandrasekhar. Looking at the
bowling line up there would be
some marathon spells ahead for
'Ram' and 'Val'.

Above: Jack Fingleton
had to show Taurean
strength of character
when facing the bodyline
bowling of 1932-33.
Left: Captain of Taurus,
Ted Dexter, would have
Valentine and
Ramadhin as his slow
bowlers.
Opposite, above: One of
the better sides, Gemini
has Denis Compton to
provide middle-of-the-
order runs.
Opposite, below:
Charming and with a
desire to express himself
describes the Gemini
type, and Tom Graveney
could hardly be a better
example.

114

Gemini

22 May to
21 June

Harmonious signs
Aquarius, Libra

The Geminian is a charming type with many friends, impatient with repetition and with a great desire to express himself. Denis Compton, John Reid, Brian Statham and Derek Underwood look like typical Gemini characters.

EDRICH, J.H. England
GRAVENEY, T.W. England
HEADLEY, G.A. West Indies
COMPTON, D.C.S. England
REID, J.R. New Zealand
DAVIDSON, A.K. Australia
*ILLINGWORTH, R. England
†GRIFFITH, S.C. England
TYSON, F.H. England
UNDERWOOD, D.L. England
STATHAM, J.B. England

Gemini has a truly magnificent eleven which would take a lot of beating. Tyson, Statham, Davidson followed by Underwood and Illingworth is any captain's dream of a bowling side.

Cancer

22 June to
22 July

Harmonious signs
Pisces, Scorpio, Taurus

The Cancerian can be summed up in one word: patience, a word which would apply equally to Hutton, Gavaskar, Bedser and Bob Taylor. He also loves a large audience, a view to which Rowan, Lock and Lillee must inevitably subscribe.

*HUTTON, L. England
RICHARDS, B.A. S. Africa
GAVASKAR, S.M. India
ROWAN, E.A. South Africa
McLEAN, R.A. South Africa
†TAYLOR, R.W. England
LOCK, G.A.R. England
BEDSER, A.V. England
McKENZIE, G.D. Australia
APPLEYARD, R. England
LILLEE, D.K. Australia

Cancer produces another excellent bowling side equipped for all types of wickets, in a team in which England can find only one top line batsman in contrast to three from South Africa.

Above: Dennis Lillee provides fire-power for Cancer.
Left: Cancer is strong in opening batsman, and Barry Richards should get them off to a fast start.
Opposite, above: Roy Tattersall provides off-spin for Leo.
Opposite, below left: Greg Chappell, one of several Test captains born under Leo.
Opposite, below right: Godfrey Evans, Leo's keeper, compares joints with Arthur McIntyre, fellow wicket-keeper.

Leo

23 July to
23 August

Harmonious signs
Sagittarius,
Aries

The Leonian types are the organisers who understand and appreciate the qualities of all other types. Consequently they make good leaders. Five of the batsmen have excelled as captains, while anyone who toured with Godfrey Evans would hardly doubt his organising ability.

BARLOW, E.J. S. Africa
GODDARD, T.L. S. Africa
CHAPPELL, G.S. Australia
ZAHEER ABBAS Pakistan
*SOBERS, G.A. West Indies
ATKINSON, D.E. West Indies
†EVANS, T.G. England
VOCE, W. England
TATTERSALL, R. England
THOMSON, J.R. Australia
WRIGHT, D.V.P. England

There is not a single English batsman born a Leo good enough 'to be included in a side which can boast five players as genuine all-rounders.

117

Virgo

24 August to
23 September

Harmonious signs
Capricorn, Taurus

The Virgo type separates, sifts, classifies and arranges his materials and his men, recognising at a glance the potential value of each, and making the best of everyone and everything. 'The Don' could only have been a Virgo.

SOLOMON, J.S. West Indies
HASSETT, A.L. Australia
*BRADMAN, D.G. Australia
LLOYD, C.H. West Indies
PROCTOR, M.J. South Africa
BUTCHER, B.F. West Indies
PEPPER, C.G. New South Wales
†LANGLEY, G.R.A. Australia
HALL, W.W. West Indies
ARNOLD, G.G. England
WALKER, M.H.N. Australia

Virgo is the only team to include an uncapped cricketer but Cec Pepper undoubtedly would have made his mark in the highest company if he had remained in his native Australia. Any team containing 'The Don' at number three would be difficult to overcome, and just look whom he has in support.

Above: Virgo is rich in seamers and fast bowlers, among them Mike Procter who also provides batting power.
Left: Captain of Virgo, Don Bradman.
Opposite, above: Libra is my idea of the strongest and best-balanced team. Bishan Bedi teams with Lance Gibbs for the slow bowling stints.
Opposite, below: The fast bowling is well looked after. John Snow (*left*) has what he often lacked in his career, a class partner, and they do not come classier than Ray Lindwall (*right*).

Libra

24 September to
23 October

Harmonious signs
Aquarius, Gemini

The Libran type who succeeds in life is generally in one way or another a specialist. You can say that again!

PONSFORD, W.H. Australia
BOYCOTT, G. England
HARVEY, R.N. Australia
CHAPPELL, I.M. Australia
GREIG, A.W. England
† PARKS, J.M. England
*BENAUD, R. Australia
LINDWALL, R.R. Australia
SNOW, J.A. England
GIBBS, L.R. West Indies
BEDI, B.S. India

In a Libran side which has a perfectly balanced attack no place could be found for three excellent all-rounders in Basil D'Oliveira, George Tribe and Gerry Gomez. Little wonder that the Librans would carry my money in any competition.

Scorpio

24 October to
22 November
Harmonious signs
Cancer, Pisces

The Scorpion is reputed to be strong, powerful and muscular with a thick set frame, characteristics which certainly apply to six of my team. Interesting that the slightly built Peter Loader, born on 25 October, is a borderline case.

SUTCLIFFE, B. New Zealand
McDONALD, C.C. Australia
*NOURSE, A.D.S. Africa
NURSE, S.M. West Indies
MUSHTAQ, M. Pakistan
MACKAY, K.D. Australia
ARCHER, R.G. Australia
†MARSH, R.W. Australia
DOOLAND, B. Australia
LARWOOD, H. England
LOADER, P.J. England

Genuine pace, two wrist spinners and left and right-handed stroke makers combine to make the Scorpions a sight to warm the cockles of Jim Swanton's heart.

Above: Dudley Nourse, South African captain and fine batsman, is my choice to captain the Scorpio side.
Left: Harold Larwood will keep Scorpio's opponents on edge. Bill Woodfull is ducking below this thunderbolt.
Opposite, above: Tiger O'Reilly provides aggressive spin bowling for Sagittarius.
Opposite, below: Two great all-rounders, who were keen opponents on the field, join forces for Sagittarius, Keith Miller (*left*) and Trevor Bailey.

Sagittarius

23 November to
21 December

Harmonious signs
Aries, Leo

The Sagittarian is universally acclaimed to be a sportsman. He shows a predilection for outdoor work. Certainly none of the above has become desk bound in retirement.

WASHBROOK, C. England
HANIF MOHAMMAD Pakistan
BARRINGTON, K.F. England
† AMES, L.E.G. England
MILLER, K.R. Australia
WALTERS, K.D. Australia
*BAILEY, T.E. England
BOTHAM, I.T. England
TITMUS, F.J. England
O'REILLY, W.J. Australia
GRIFFITH, C.C. West Indies

Dependable Barrington and Bailey, the defiance of Hanif together with the flair of Miller, Walters and Ames suggests the Sagittarians would have the answer to any kind of playing conditions. So indeed would the great variety of their attack.

SUMMARY

England thus supplied 46 cricketers of whom approximately one quarter were born in the heart of the summer under the signs of Gemini and Cancer. Australia on the other hand provided five Aquarians and five Librans, almost one third of their 34 representatives, whilst Taurus and Virgo claimed eight of the 22 West Indians.

To add a final touch, and really throw myself wide open to every would-be selector, I have selected one representative from each star sign to complete a world eleven, added a twelfth man and then picked a further five players to undertake a world tour. The final result is as follows:

World Eleven	Twelfth Man
HUTTON, L. Cancer	DEXTER, E.R. Taurus
MORRIS, A.R. Capricorn	
*BRADMAN, D.G. Virgo	Extra five for touring party
COMPTON, D.C.S. Gemini	EVANS, T.G. Leo
WEEKES, E.D. Pisces	BEDSER, A.V. Cancer
SOBERS, G.A. Leo	RICHARDS, I.V.A. Pisces
BENAUD, R. Libra	LINDWALL, R.R. Libra
†KNOTT, A.P.E. Aries	LAKER, J.C. Aquarius
LARWOOD, H. Scorpio	
TRUEMAN, F.S. Aquarius	
O'REILLY, W.J. Sagittarius	

I can only apologise for the last named, but I am certainly not going to miss out on such a tour.

According to the stars, if one is looking for perfect harmony during this tour of fantasy there should be no problem arising in the allocations of rooms. Compatible and harmonious signs would result in the following pairings:

BRADMAN (Capt) Single	SOBERS and RICHARDS
HUTTON and LARWOOD	BENAUD and TRUEMAN
MORRIS and DEXTER	KNOTT and O'REILLY
COMPTON and EVANS	LAKER and LINDWALL
WEEKES and BEDSER	

The ideal manager should come from amongst the Virgo types, and with Bradman already committed as captain the ideal choice would surely be Lindsay Hassett. It is also said that the types to run any business come from the signs of Leo, Cancer and Taurus. Our tour committee therefore would consist of the Manager and Captain along with Hutton, Dexter and Sobers.

Arthur Morris is the Capricorn choice to open with Len Hutton in my World Eleven. Here he is batting in an Adelaide Test match, and getting the ball through the untenanted gully.

Captain of the World Eleven, Don Bradman. In the Nottingham Test of 1938 he is seen turning a ball to leg. Les Ames watches.

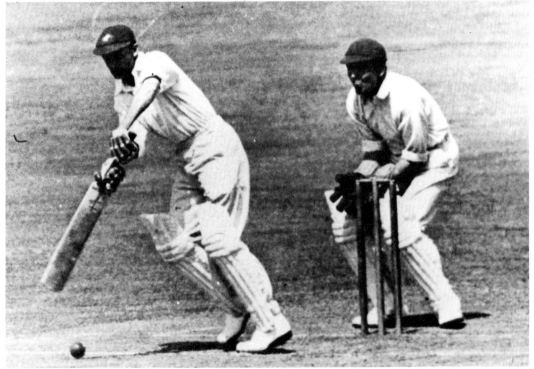

Umpires

There are periods when English Test match cricketers are very much in the ascendancy, and conversely, of course, there are the bad times when one begins to wonder if we shall ever again produce players to match the skills of past heroes. The same cannot be said of English umpires. Year in and year out they appear to remain in a class of their own and certainly as far as I can remember have constantly reached far higher standards and a greater degree of accuracy than their counterparts in other countries.

There is no substitute for experience and with few exceptions English umpires are drawn from the ranks of ex-professional cricketers who have spent long informative years in the middle. Each decade in English cricket seems to produce at least one outstanding umpire, and these have included in my time the names of Frank Chester, Frank Lee, Syd Buller, Charles Elliott and Harold Bird. All of them were excellent players in their own right and I am sure that the majority of their decisions have been based on their knowledge of the game as participants rather than hours spent studying the law books.

At the other end of the scale there were naturally several eminent ex-cricketers who never measured up to requirements. With more cricket played in this country than anywhere else in the world a sub-standard umpire is quickly found out and rapidly discarded. No umpire can possibly claim to be perfect; they all make mistakes as all humans do, but the better ones are very simply those who make the fewest errors. Maybe I was more fortunate than some (disregarding those batsmen who think they are never out) but in a career spanning some 16 English summers I believe there were no more than half a dozen occasions when I felt that I had been harshly treated as a batsman. Possibly as a bowler there were a few more!

Frank Chester will always remain firmly at the top of my umpires table. A brilliant prospect as a batsman, he had made four centuries for Worcestershire at the age of 18, including an undefeated 178. Tragically he lost his right hand in the First World War and at the age of 26 he turned to umpiring as a full-time career. He set new standards and changed the whole conception of what an umpire should be. He officiated in 48 Tests during his 33 years in the long white coat. As a raw recruit to the first class game I recall asking him

Cyril Washbrook out caught Tallon bowled Miller at the start of an England innings against Australia in 1948. The greatest of all umpires Frank Chester has his finger raised.

one day if it was true that umpires gave the benefit of the doubt to the batsmen. He looked positively shaken. 'Doubt,' he said, 'there never is any doubt.'

In a Test match at Leeds one day against Australia I tried to hook a bouncer from Keith Miller but succeeded only in getting the slightest of deflections from my glove through to the wicket keeper. I barely felt it; in fact it was such a faint touch that not one of the 11 Australians offered any sort of appeal. That in itself must have been a record of some kind. A couple of minutes later when I was the non-striker down at Frank's end he turned to me and whispered out of the corner of his mouth 'You were a lucky lad'. Oddly enough that Test was just about the beginning of the end for him. He was a sick man and made several mistakes which were completely out of character. It was not long before he had to retire due to ill health and it was a sad day for many of us when he died in 1957 aged 61.

125

One could not say that Alec Skelding ever reached the same heights as an umpire but one could safely say that there was never a more popular or beloved character on the circuit. His sharp wit amused us all through long hard days, and Alec had plenty of those during his 27 years on the list. Chosen to officiate in the University match at Lord's one year during a hot and sticky spell of weather he was not slow in expressing his feelings about a scoring rate of some thirty runs per hour. It was indeed hot enough for drinks to be brought out in mid-afternoon. The University twelfth man approached Alec clutching an orange juice in one hand and a lemonade in the other to ask him his preference. 'Nay lad', said Alec, 'did you not bring out any stomach powder, this cricket's giving me the belly ache'.

At the age of 71 he finally umpired his last game, and two years later I happened to be in his home town of Leicester one March evening and made my way round to Alec's favourite hostelry. He appeared within minutes as if from nowhere and we spent an uproarious evening in the company of his cronies. I was so glad that I had tracked him down again when within a month I read that he had died.

Frank Lee and Charles Elliott were not unlike as cricketers. Both were solid, determined, reliable openers, characteristics which they

Left: My old friend from wartime days in the Middle East, Sam Pothecary, concentrating hard as I send one down for Surrey.
Right: Frank Lee (*left*) and Syd Buller walking out to officiate in a Test match at Edgbaston in 1961.

brought into their umpiring lives. In the middle both were ready for a chat and a joke but woe betide anyone who attempted to pull a fast one.

For years I could never understand why we never had a standing umpire as a selector. So many of them knew the game inside out, they spent every day of the summer in the very heart of the game of cricket and from the best vantage point saw far more of our cricketers than the normal run of selectors. Finally Elliott was chosen as an England selector and judging by results since he became a member of the panel, the choice has been a shrewd one.

Sam Pothecary and I played a lot of war-time cricket together in the Middle East and became firm friends. As fate would have it he

Dickie Bird is today's best-known umpire, always letting the crowd know what he's doing. In this picture he is telling Wayne Daniel that he is stepping onto the pitch.

128

made his debut as an umpire in a Surrey match at the Oval, and when bowling from Sam's end I had the good fortune to pick up five wickets. When I say that three of the batsmen were caught by the wicket-keeper and the other two were dismissed lbw you can imagine the state that poor old Sam found himself in. After he had given the fifth man out he said to me 'For Pete's sake have a bowl at the other end, or if you are staying here make sure you hit the stumps. This looks like the biggest carve-up of all time'.

If Frank Chester set the standards of English umpiring then Syd Buller not only maintained them but spread the gospel far and wide. He was a Yorkshireman through and through, yet had a great love of his adopted county of Worcestershire. Always immaculately turned out with the cuffs of his white coat neatly folded back to show the gnarled hands of the ex wicket-keeper's trade and showing sufficient forearm to denote his thorough and businesslike approach to the job in hand, he became acknowledged as crickets' top umpire. He was utterly fearless and waged his own personal war on the throwing brigade of his time. He travelled the world showing his skills and lecturing on the subject he knew so well. It was a great loss to cricket when he collapsed and died suddenly when officiating at Edgbaston in August 1970.

The high standard has most certainly been maintained in the capable hands of Harold 'Dickie' Bird. Make no mistake, an umpire's job in the 1970s is far more demanding than it ever was when Frank Chester and Alec Skelding were in office. Gentlemanly attitudes have unhappily given way among the players to a new combative climate. Large financial rewards for top players have made winning so much more important. Television action replays have also given umpires additional pressures, yet out of it all Dickie Bird has emerged with flying colours. Even Dickie's best friends could not call him a quiet unobtrusive umpire, in fact many people have suggested that he goes out of his way to bring the spotlight on himself. He has certainly succeeded in that, and given the lie to the old 'W.G.' story. When the great man himself was adjudged lbw in a charity game, he told the umpire not to be so foolish, as the crowd had come to watch him bat and 'not to see you umpire'.

Those of us who know Dickie well realise how much he worries and how much he lives on his nerves. He aims to be a perfectionist in his job and certainly no other official has come closer to achieving this end. In emphasising the superiority and the high standards of our English umpires, it would be unfair to suggest that we hold a monopoly. Jamaica produced two West Indian Test umpires in Perry Burke and Tom Ewart who were of the highest class, and the same could be said of Messrs Collins and Costello in South Africa. Touring English cricketers spoke highly of the Australians Mel McInnes and Col Hoy, and if a visiting player ever sings the praises

of a home umpire you can be sure he has been completely impartial.

I am also sure that the umpires who officiated in the Australia–England series in 1978-79 were completely beyond reproach so far as their impartiality and honesty went, yet it was my opinion that the standard of umpiring fell a long way short of requirements. My judgements are not influenced by the histrionics of such colourful characters as Hogg and Botham, both of whom could have won Oscars for drama. Never in any previous series had I seen so many appeals by both sides and one could only assume that the players were working on the premise that the more you shout the higher will be the number of appeals answered in your favour. In

Above left: Charlie Elliot, a successful opening batsman in his day, and now one of the top umpires, was eventually chosen as one of England's selectors – a wise decision which paid dividends.

Above: One of the controversial decisions in the 1978-79 England tour of Australia. Umpire Tom Brooks gives Graeme Wood out caught behind by Bob Taylor off John Lever. Wood looks reluctant to go, and at the lunch interval Tom Brooks announced his retirement.

fact it probably turned out to be the case in that particular series, when I believe we reached an all time low in umpiring standards.

Normally my sympathies lie very much with the umpires. They lose the toss every day, have to endure biting cold winds one day and heat waves another day. Every decision they make is subject to close scrutiny in a job which requires 100 per cent concentration day in and day out. At long last for Test Matches in England they are finally paid a fee which is commensurate to the task they undertake. This applies to only the chosen few, and for the remainder it remains largely a labour of love, and indeed to quote once again our friend Alec Skelding they are still an 'ill-considered lot'.

131

Benefits

In 1958, Arthur Jepson the Nottinghamshire pace bowler was awarded a benefit or testimonial which amounted to £1,511, after an association with the Club of 20 years. Twenty years on it will come as no surprise to many of our cricketers if at least two of the 1978 beneficiaries will be investing sums in the region of £50,000 for their efforts. Little wonder, therefore, that a constant topic of dressing room conversation up and down the land concerns escalating benefit returns. The principal worry is whether cricket benefits will continue to remain free of tax.

A Test case over 50 years ago regarding the liability of a benefit to tax was decided in the cricketers' favour. The question that must now worry our administrators is whether the conditions relating to benefits laid down by the counties in those far off days have changed sufficiently to warrant the Inland Revenue taking a closer look. The basic condition remains the same. The benefit is an *ex gratia* payment and is uncontracted. There is no guarantee of a benefit to any player, though these days it would be unlikely that any player with ten years 'capped' service would miss out.

When the cricketers' case went to the Law Courts the *ex gratia* payment arrived from three sources, all closely connected with the game: the total revenue less expenses from one selected fixture, members' subscriptions lists, and possibly two or three ground collections. After the Second World War, this was augmented by Sunday games within the county played in aid of the beneficiary, together with a few social evenings on a fairly small scale. The start of the John Player League meant a substantial reduction in the number of vacant Sundays and cricketers began to look elsewhere to recoup the benefit losses. A popular idea was the sale of benefit ties which certainly proved financially rewarding, but to market these on a large scale would surely seriously contravene tax laws. Otherwise there would be nothing to stop the beneficiary selling shirts, flannels, boots etc, and for a year setting up as a retailer. MCC saw the danger of benefit ties and put a restriction on them. They continue to appear in a limited form purely as gifts to helpful supporters.

If benefits were to keep pace with growing inflation and increasing living costs some new and original thoughts on raising

Norman Graham was no doubt thankful that he played in a successful and well-supported Kent team when his benefit realised over £38,000.

money were necessary. The players were also being badly hit by falling gates. Previously they had been the chief source for the beneficiary, but by the late 1960s gate receipts for a three-day county match would barely cover expenses. Thus we entered the era of sponsored celebrity golf competitions, soccer matches, motor car raffles, public house lotteries, dinner dances and cabaret evenings. All these events were run on professional lines by loyal and dedicated committees. It is no exaggeration to say that a recent sponsored golf competition played on behalf of an international cricketer, in which I was privileged to take part, raised £10,000 in a single day.

One of the most fascinating aspects of the question of benefits is a comparison of published figures in the 20-year period between the wars and the 30 years since cricket was resumed in 1946. One must consider, of course, the depression and general strike in the late 1920s, the extremely low wages and vast number of unemployed, yet as the country gradually became more affluent in the 1930s it was hardly reflected in benefit figures. In those days Yorkshire was

the place to have a benefit. The popular Roy Kilner netted £4,000 in 1925, whilst his counterpart in the 1930s, Maurice Leyland, received £3,600 in 1934. These were exceptional amounts, and the average in those pre-war years was more likely to be on a par with the £1,200 received by Leslie Ames in 1937. If therefore, there was little significant change in the pre-war period the same could not be said of figures published in post-war years. The following table, compiled from the figures published, gives a general idea of the upward trend.

Right: Cyril Washbrook (*right*) also opening with Len Hutton, was the recipient of £14,000 in 1948, worth several times more by today's standards.

Average Benefits

1953	£4,200*	1961	£4,450	1973	£10,677
1954	£2,940	1963	£5,413	1974	£12,840
1955	£3,082	1964	£6,469	1975	£16,591
1956	£3,694	1968	£7,315		
1957	£3,934	1972	£8,334		

*Alec Bedser's £13,000 benefit greatly improved the average take.

Left: Les Jackson, unlucky to play for unfashionable Derbyshire. His benefit of £2,900 was worth only £1·76 per wicket.
Above: Mike Brearley's benefit in 1978 is expected to break the record and be well in excess of £40,000, tax-free.

Dennis Brookes (*left*) and John Langridge (*right*), opening batsmen for Northants and Sussex respectively, received less than £4,000 each for their benefits in the 1950s. Between them the two batsmen had played for over 50 years and scored over 65,000 runs.

Since this table was compiled Ray Illingworth and Norman Graham have returned benefit figures in excess of £38,000, Brian Close was not far behind with £35,000, and Clive Lloyd, Farokh Engineer and Alan Knott netted amounts of £27,119, £26,159 and £27,037 respectively.

If reports coming in from Hove and Lords are indeed accurate then the benefits awarded to Peter Graves and Mike Brearley in 1978 will establish all time records. Thus in the last 20 years the average cricketers' benefit will have risen from a round figure of £4,000 to somewhere in the region of £30,000, tax free of course. On the face of it the rewards may be considered by many people to have escalated too high. This kind of thinking has also entered the minds of a number of our players who are concerned that the Inland Revenue may well take a long hard look at all cricketers' benefits. In view of the purchasing power of the pound sterling in 1979, compared to that of 20 to 30 years ago, it is not an opinion that I share. One could argue that Maurice Leyland's benefit of £3,600 in 1934 was worth considerably more than the £20,639 received by Geoffrey Boycott exactly 40 years later. The great Yorkshire left-hander could comfortably have purchased at least half a dozen most desirable properties, and goodness knows what they would be worth on the open market today. Similarly Cyril Washbrook's £14,000 benefit in 1948 must be worth much more than the combined sums raised in Lancashire by Clive Lloyd and Farokh Engineer. Strictly

137

on this kind of parallel the present day international cricketer is certainly not rewarded any better than the players of previous eras.

However, are benefits today earned the hard way, as they surely were in days gone by? Several counties it would seem have signed top cricketing stars by dangling the carrot of a tax-free benefit far in advance of the normally accepted period. Gary Sobers was given a Nottinghamshire benefit at the beginning of only his fifth season with them, while Brian Close at Somerset had only to survive a year longer before collecting £35,000. Bear in mind too that Close had previously received both a benefit and a testimonial with Yorkshire which amounted to £14,695.

If one considers that Joe Hardstaff played for Nottinghamshire for 25 years, scored 31,847 runs and made 83 centuries, then his testimonial of £1,361 in 1953 was beggarly. Dennis Brookes carried the Northamptonshire batting for a similar period of time, scoring 30,874 runs and 71 centuries, only to receive £3,280 in 1958 and John Langridge, after 27 years with Sussex, had a benefit in 1953 worth £3,825. He, incidentally, had scored 34,380 runs which included 76 hundreds.

Of course there always has been a fair amount of luck attached to these benefits; luck concerning weather, personal performances and the cricket interest of a particular season. At one time also much depended on the affluence and success of the county, though the differential these days has narrowed considerably. Players of Yorkshire, Lancashire, Surrey and Middlesex at one time had a great advantage over players from such as Derbyshire, Northants and Nottinghamshire. If Les Jackson had played for one of the first-named counties it would be odds on that his benefit would have realised more than £2,900. Big Leslie took 1,733 wickets, which means that each victim was worth £1.67 to him. Norman Graham of Kent could never be considered in the same league as an opening bowler, yet the enthusiastic support of the Kent public brought him at least £38,214 for his 613 wickets. That works out at £62 a victim!

These I believe to be the injustices of the benefit system. Have a look at the career of Bob Cottam, voted the best young cricketer of the year in 1968. He played the best part of nine seasons with Hampshire, followed by another four years with Northants, captured 1,010 wickets and played four times for England, yet there is no record of his receiving anything more than a meagre annual wage for his efforts. This, I suppose just about puts him on a par with that most endearing of cricket characters, Alec Skelding, Leicestershire bowler and umpire for so many years. When drawn on the subject of his benefit he simply said 'Play began before a keen wind'. After a further ten years and a thousand overs a season he was offered a second benefit. 'It is very kind of you' said Alec, 'but I just can't afford it'.

Bob Cottam, whose benefit could hardly have been smaller, as he wasn't awarded one. Thirteen years' bowling for over 1,000 wickets isn't enough in some circumstances.

138

The Unfinished Packer Saga

The majority opinion on the whole Packer saga is that World Series Cricket was developed as a result of the Australian Board of Control's refusal to grant him exclusive rights to televise cricket on his own Channel 9. He had, in fact discussed the idea of launching his own international cricket series with his executives some three years earlier, and the Board's decision was really the last straw that broke the camel's back.

Strangely enough the English cricket authorities had agreed with Packer that he should televise the 1977 series with Australia, much against the wishes of their Australian counterparts. He thus had one foot in the door, and decided to go ahead on a scale no one could possibly have imagined. In May 1977 the cricket world was stunned and rocked to its foundations when the plans to set up a new form of cricket were unfolded. Suddenly the name of Kerry Packer was on the lips of every cricket follower from Bradford to Barbados and from Delhi to Durban – few, if any, knew much about him.

His grandfather raised his fare from Tasmania to Sydney by virtue of a winning horse on the race track. His father, Sir Frank Packer, starting as a young reporter, became one of Australia's legendary Press barons, building a massive newspaper empire before turning to television. When Kerry finally took over on the death of his father in 1974, he more than doubled the company's assets as head of a vast multi-million dollar conglomerate. He still found enough time to become an accomplished golfer and to play a reasonable game of tennis. An enthusiastic game hunter and fisherman and a keen supporter of rugby league, there is little evidence that he was connected in any way with the game of cricket. Why then had he suddenly become obsessed with marketing this most intricate of sports?

Obviously his anger with ACB was a prime reason, and as a bystander he appeared to me to have a good case. As a business man he felt he could make money and as a fiercely partisan Australian he was looking to professionalise the game in Australia, to make it a worthwhile living for the leading players and to attempt to put their earnings on a par with the leading golfers and tennis players he knew so much better. Rightly or wrongly I have felt that if success could have come his way he would have limited the exercise to his own kith and kin, but of course he needed the support of other nationalities and to do this he found a ready lieutenant in Tony Greig.

Before I move into the Greig story may I say that on reflection this new cricket revolution should not really have been such a complete surprise. For years one had listened to dressing room murmurs on low pay and poor conditions; the ideas of a players union and privately organised games and tours were being mooted 30 years ago. I, for one, have never been opposed to the type of cricket now

set in motion by Kerry Packer but at the same time I took a violent
objection to the underhand manner in which it was announced and
introduced in May 1977 and in which, from the English point of
view, Tony Greig, England's captain played the lead.

Never at any stage had I criticised Tony Greig as an England
cricketer or indeed on his appointment as England's captain. With
the demise of the unfortunate and unlucky Denness, he was a
natural for the job and brought to England's Test Match scene a
flair and charisma which made him both popular and successful.
His record for England as captain, as batsman and indeed as bowler
was beyond reproach. He spent the winter of 1976-76 in Sydney
most lucratively and no one could blame him for that, yet prior to
his return in 1976 I sensed that he felt his future lay 'down under'; in
fact he announced his intention of returning to Sydney the following
winter despite the fact that MCC were due to tour India. I took him
to task in the *Daily Express*, querying his statement that he was not
certain to be selected for India and suggesting that as England's
captain his first priority should be to English cricket. He was

incensed with my article and was allowed to reply in the paper the following week. In the strongest possible manner he refuted any insinuation I might have made, going on to say what an honour it was to be England's captain and that if selected he would be ready and willing to tour India. Most important of all he went on to say that he would seek approval from Lord's for any decisions he might make regarding his future and keep them informed. Within twelve months he had played a leading part in secret negotiations which could do nothing but harm to the very people he had earlier promised to support.

From the moment the story broke Tony was hounded from pillar to post by the press and television. He is a very good and plausible speaker and persuaded many that what he had done was for the benefit of cricket and cricketers in general, emphasising time and again that the benefit would be felt by the lowest paid player in the poorest county side. No one would argue that WSC has greatly improved the financial lot of the chosen few, but I would take a lot of convincing that cricketers such as John Barclay of Sussex, David Acfield of Essex or Harry Pilling of Lancashire are any better off. There was little doubt that Greig had sold himself body and soul to Kerry Packer, had sworn allegiance that there would be no leak until the appropriate time and I was equally sure that Packer would stand firmly by Greig. By the same token I am sure that if Lord's had been fully in the picture as promised by Greig, they would have attempted to find a solution, though they would have met fierce resistance from the Australian Cricket Board, who it seemed would not concede an inch of the way.

For all of us closely connected with the game it was decision time – time to be counted as pro or anti Packer. Hard as I searched and hoped for some sort of compromise, it seemed inevitable after a while that one was not forthcoming, and nobody can lay the blame fully for this on Packer's shoulders. Due totally to the underhand manner in which establishment cricket had been stabbed in the back, I opted to stay with the people who had provided me with a life full of excitement, great joy and world travel, and who had made me the envy of so many people. Having declared myself I was invited by David Frost to face Kerry Packer on the 'Frost Programme', an event I was looking forward to. It seemed to me an admirable opportunity to discuss seriously and intelligently the whole complex situation and secretly I nurtured the thought that some good might come of it.

These hopes were dashed when Robin Marlar arrived on the scene to make up the quartet. Robin had been a good friend of mine ever since he was captain and I coach to Cambridge University. He had tremendous potential as an off spin bowler but never quite reached the heights that his ability warranted. For many years now he has been in the top flight of cricket journalists and is certainly the first one I turn to when the Sunday papers, industrial disputes permitting, arrive on the mat. Periodically, he has an outburst, either verbally or in print, and unhappily he chose the Frost programme for one of them. His temper reached boiling point as he confronted Kerry Packer, he completely lost his self control and he was quietly and clinically taken apart by the cool professionalism of Packer. Worst of all he received little sympathy from David Frost and none at all from the studio audience, the majority of whom probably believed that I ran an airline! In the end all I could do was to attempt to bring some calmness and common sense to the proceedings and the programme ended with K.P. winning by an innings.

At least the evening gave me an opportunity for a fairly lengthy chat with the Australian tycoon which revolved principally on his thoughts on television coverage for his forthcoming series. The use of eight cameras (as compared to four that the BBC normally use) with

Fred Trueman, a forthright English bowler and a forthright commentator, who changed his style when commenting on WSC matches on Channel 9.

two cameras in action at both ends showed that no expense would be spared. With a wry smile he hinted that he would like me to be involved as a commentator. If it was possible I produced an even wryer smile in return. Within a few days and thanks to a recommendation of Richie Benaud, a most lucrative offer was handed to me by my agent. In essence his terms to me for roughly an eight-week engagement in Australia were approximately the equivalent of a full three-year contract with the BBC.

Often I have been asked whether or not, had I been at the peak of my career when this cricket revolution arrived, I would have accepted the terms offered. Without being too dogmatic I do not believe that I would. Now, it took me less than 24 hours to thank him for his kind offer and decline it without offering a reason. Fred Trueman, who had been waiting anxiously in the wings, accepted the offer with alacrity. I further knew that there would be no monetary compensation coming my way as a result of my decision,

146

as of course was the case when several of our players and indeed our leading umpire turned their backs on WSC.

If I harboured any doubts as to the wisdom of the action I had taken, they quickly disappeared when I visited Australia in the winter of 1978-79. I could not have been a party to the loaded, biased, non-critical commentary which I listened to for many hours on Channel 9.

It had taken some little time before it became apparent to most people the part that my friend and television colleague Richie Benaud had played, and indeed was still playing, in the formation and organisation of Packer-style cricket. Richie had done his best to avoid publicity and had kept a very low profile on the whole situation. When quizzed on the part he was playing he would go no further than saying that his company had been approached in their capacity of public relations consultants by Kerry Packer and they had agreed to act for him.

At this stage let me say that I have the greatest admiration for Richie. He was a magnificent cricketer, in my view the best captain Australia have produced during my time, and that included Sir Donald Bradman. As a cricket commentator he is far ahead of anyone I have heard in any part of the world, and never have I met a more industrious, hard-working yet generous ex-cricketer in my career.

The contracts offered to the players by Packer are there for all to see ranging from the A$40,000 for the three years offered to Tony Greig down to A$16,500 for one year to Ian Redpath, yet never has there been a figure published for the Benaud contract. It must surely have been out of this world and not for one minute would I criticise Richie for accepting it. For that matter also I believe that each and every player that Kerry Packer signed had a right to make his own decision, provided he was completely aware of what it might entail. Benaud's cricketing advice to Packer was to prove invaluable, particularly in respect of the players who were offered contracts and his insistence that WSC had to be played as strictly as possible to the laws of the established game. Here he met some resistance from several of the non-cricketing executives who would have been happier to overrule some of the finer and acknowledged points of the game in favour of the razzamatazz of a wandering road show. Happily on most counts Benaud had his own way.

Of course in accepting the appointment Richie lost many friends. He was blackballed by the ACB and his great friend and room-mate for so long, Neil Harvey, just about disowned him, and he also received pretty short shrift from Sir Donald Bradman. For years he had been welcomed by one and all in England, yet while he still retained the friendship of a good percentage of Englishmen (myself included) there remained a good many who cut him dead. Indeed the unhappiest feature in cricket since Kerry Packer appeared on the scene is the sudden ending of life-long friendships, which since cricket was first played have been a pleasant feature of cricketers' lives.

If I have spotlighted Tony Greig and Richie Benaud in this chapter, that I must add the name of Derek Underwood, for his defection to WSC was possibly the one signing which surprised and upset cricket followers at home most of all. If you have seen him scores of times on a cricket field, then you would find him exactly as you would expect, should you come to spend any time in his company. Honest, decent, straightforward and English through and through, with a burning desire to play cricket for Kent and England. He was a hundred per cent trier, who never failed to give of his best. In an interview in the *Daily Express* Derek stated his reasons for accepting the Packer offer as follows: 'I have sensed that people consider me a pirate, a rebel, a money grabber and worse, when in reality all I'm trying to do is to achieve a degree of security for my wife and two daughters. I have no other qualifications once my career is over and up to now I have been unable to save much on my income.'

His newly signed contract was reputed to be worth A$25,000 for three years. His reasoning to many may well have been acceptable, but to me it smacked of pessimism and a certain lack of ambition. Sir Leonard Hutton, Denis Compton and Ken Barrington all left school at fourteen and had gone into full-time cricket without qualifications. Were the two years spent as a clerk in a solicitor's office qualifications for Alec Bedser's future? One could go on and on and quote many other examples. Also do not forget that Derek had in 1975 pocketed a tax free benefit worth £25,000. Derek signed his allegiance to Kerry Packer and despite several entreaties to him has remained loyal to WSC. Ironically, if he had remained with established cricket his earnings, as things have turned out, would now be in excess of his present contract, he would have broken every wicket-taking record in Test cricket and he would, I am sure, have been much happier bowling at Brisbane under Mike Brearley than making the long trek home from VFL Park in Melbourne close to midnight each day.

There seemed just a hope that a compromise might be reached when in June the quartet of Packer, Benaud, McNicoll and Taylor arrived at Lord's for further discussion with the ICC. 'Tadge' Webster, as chairman, produced five points around which it was felt a compromise could be effected. To most people's surprise, Packer agreed that he would compromise on all those counts, and for his part in return he would ask for no victimisation of his signed players and once again television rights for the series after the

Deadly Derek. Of all the players who signed for Packer I think Derek Underwood made the biggest mistake. His decision was too cautious, and had he remained with established cricket his future could have been much brighter.

conclusion of ABC's contract. He would of course pay handsomely for them. Messrs Parish and Steele, the Australian representatives, would never submit to this bargaining and with increasing support for them round the table the meeting ended with an angry Packer striding out to face a barrage of journalists with what was a declaration of cricket war.

I believed all along that the players should be allowed to make decisions for themselves, and personally I had no axe to grind with the representatives of English cricket, Messrs Amiss, Greig, Knott, Woolmer, Underwood and Snow, who had joined the Packer organisation. Equally, however, there was absolutely no way I would have employed them or any of their overseas colleagues in English cricket once their present contracts were ended. With open war now declared and cricket being run very much on business lines by two rival organisations, I could not possibly understand how one could work six months for one side and six months for the other. There cannot be many people who spend six months working for Gillette and the rest of the year with Wilkinson Sword!

By and large the counties in England would not take such drastic action, with the possible exceptions of Kent and Warwickshire. The first named in the end got cold feet, after stating that they would not renew the Packer players contracts. It possibly occurred to them that without Knott, Underwood, Woolmer, Asif, Julien and co their chances of winning would diminish and the Kent crowds have become as fiercely partisan as ever were Surrey and Yorkshire.

I suppose in many ways Packer was unlucky that Australian Test cricket standards were at an all time low when he made his grab. The 1977 side under Greg Chappell were a very ordinary lot and never before this century had England on their own soil had such a convincing victory. Packer signed no less than 13 of this well-beaten party of whom only two or three could be considered to be top-class performers. If he had been able to cast his net a few years ago, just think the haul that might so easily have come his way. Morris, McDonald, Davidson, Chappell and Benaud were all 33 years of age and in their cricket prime when they retired, whilst Bob Cowper, after a triple Test century, played his last Test at the age of 28. The only significant English signing was Derek Underwood – it was hardly likely that the Australian public would flock to see Amiss and Woolmer in action, and fine performer that Alan Knott has always been, crowds simply do not roll up to applaud a wicket-keeper.

With the West Indians, and the South Africans Richards and Procter, it was different. The very nature of the way cricket was played in their countries made them cricket mercenaries in the true sense of the word. Batting of the class of Lloyd, Viv and Barry Richards, and pace bowling of the calibre of Holding, Roberts and

Daniel would make these players the real draw cards.

I did not see any World Series Cricket in its first season of 1977-78 and consequently would not wish to comment too much, though I was more than surprised that so few people bothered to watch it. The average gate per day for the WSC Tests was 5,311 (including a handsome number of freeloaders) yet for the Australia – India Test the average daily attendance was 11,540. The only real success in terms of spectator interest was the floodlit cricket played at Melbourne's VFL Park, where an average of 14,818 for the four night matches was recorded. Kerry Packer had stated earlier in the year that he needed a daily average of 15,000 to break even, hence his losses in the first year were enormous. This did not seem to alarm him unduly but rather made him all the more determined to set the balance sheet right when his second season began. The obvious step was to cut the number of so-called Super Tests and place the emphasis more on the one-day floodlit games.

I arrived in Sydney on Tuesday, 28 November 1978, the very day that heralded World Series Cricket's first ever floodlit limited-over game on the Sydney Cricket Ground. This was the day that Kerry Packer had waited for for so long and he was determined to show the world that given the same facilities accorded to establishment cricket, he could prove beyond doubt that the Australian public would support him. Support him indeed they did and by 8 o'clock that evening 50,000 had responded to the press and media campaign which must have cost a fortune during the preceding week. It was by no means the normal Sydney crowd, in fact the members' enclosure was semi-deserted. A large percentage were schoolchildren and many thousands more with little knowledge of the game had come for a night out. I had not previously heard four leg byes greeted with the same sort of applause that came the way of a Richards cover drive!

For a little while I sat in the holy of holies, the private box of the Trustees, as a guest of my old friend Arthur Morris. Arthur, who had recently survived the purge of the Sydney Cricket Ground Trustees, is of course no supporter of WSC, yet was man enough to admit that this day had been an immense success for the opposition. Interestingly his last words to me were 'You know, cricket is what we all live for. Crowds and big crowds are vital to our game, and if this sort of cricket is going to pull them in, we should not discount or discredit it.'

The day was a one-off occasion; less than half of that crowd turned up the following day and nothing like it has been reached since. Yet in its second season, having learned many lessons from the previous year, WSC is showing quite spectacular advances in attendance figures. I write these words as the WSC season reaches its half-way point, and roughly 340,000 have watched the 33 games already completed, with receipts in excess of £400,000. This is somewhere around the figure for the first full season. It certainly seemed to me that there are two entirely different sets of spectators and supporters watching cricket in Australia. WSC caters for and appeals to the under-30s, many still at school, who are lured by the bright lights of night cricket, the big names and the razzamatazz which engulfs the whole exercise. It is difficult to say whether they will be permanent converts or whether the novelty will soon wear off.

In addition to watching the two Sydney matches I spent a couple of days at Melbourne's VFL Park watching more Packer cricket, and staying at the Old Melbourne Hotel where the cricketers and administrators were housed. My first reaction was that the players were certainly earning their money. I watched them in groups leaving the Hotel soon after 9 am each morning en route to some sort of promotional work prior to making the 20-mile journey out to VFL Park. Net practice preceeded an early snack lunch before play began at 1.30 pm. A short tea break at 3.30 is followed with play until 6 pm, when the players adjourn for their one long break of the day. This lasts for one hour to coincide with the switch from daylight to night cricket and the players then have a chance for their principal meal of the day. Finally comes the long uninterrupted session of three and a half hours from 7 pm to stumps at 10.30 pm. By the time the players have showered, changed and made the long drive back to base it is close to midnight.

Naturally I wondered what sort of reception would come my way, remembering that I was a home establishment figure in the middle of the enemy camp. I need not have worried; there was no enmity, no question of ill-feeling whatsoever – and surprise, surprise I even had an excellent and friendly breakfast with Tony Greig. As I have emphasised previously there had never been an occasion when I criticised any player for signing for Kerry Packer and possibly they had a measure of respect for my own decision. The cricketers themselves had not changed overnight from 'Gubby's good guys' to 'Packer Pirates'. There was no doubt that they all now knew their commitments. There would be no turning back and to a man they remained totally loyal to Kerry Packer and WSC.   Attempting to watch WSC with an impartial yet professional eye, I found it very difficult to become enthusiastic about it. The labelling of the majority of the matches was difficult to comprehend. How could I watch a side masquerading under the title of World XI which contained not a single West Indian cricketer? I did not believe there was any rigging of the games and I am sure the players were all giving of their best but possibly subconsciously that extra bit of needle was missing. It was hard to believe that Dennis Lillee could bowl ten consecutive overs without a bouncer, and it seemed to me

The Chappell Brothers, Ian at the near end and Greg, retired from Test cricket and joined Packer later. They are the backbone of WSC Australia's batting.

that the boundaries were suddenly foreshortened if the games were played on a slow outfield. The contest which certainly caught the imagination of the public and which in my view was far and away the best entertainment was the clash between Australia and the West Indies. They cannot of course go on playing each other every other day and this must be one of the aspects which is most worrying to WSC.

There is no doubt that night cricket in Australia is a brilliant Packer innovation and has come to stay. The Australian Cricket Board must be giving it a good hard look, and before long will be looking to cash in themselves. I also believe that the use of the white cricket ball was another innovation which worldwide cricket authorities should seriously consider. In texture it is no different to the old red ball and simply requires dying the leather white instead of red. The players I spoke to agreed that its performance is virtually

153

identical to the accepted ball, it retains its shine and gives the same degree of swing and movement off the pitch. There was the worry that a white ball would quickly become dirty, particularly on a rain-affected pitch or outfield, but apparently this snag was overcome. The umpires carried a spray in their pocket which immediately removed any mark or dirt and kept the ball nearly snow white in colour. VFL Park is a vast stadium yet from the furthest point from the centre it was still possible to follow fully the flight of this white ball. It would surely be a boon on a dusky English day.

For some time I had listened to the plaudits being handed around to the Television Production Team of Channel 9, and during my stay in Australia I took the opportunity of settling myself in front of the television screen for many long hours to judge for myself. Let me say the pictures were excellent, and the producer has a good deal more scope to give vent to his technique and imagination if he has eight cameras to play with. With two cameras at each end of the ground it was possible for the first time in television coverage of cricket to watch the whole action from behind the bowler's arm. In other words it was like sitting in the Lord's pavilion when the bowling was from that end and suddenly being transported to the opposite end to watch the next over from the nursery end. Of course this gives a much clearer view of the action when the batsman and possibly the wicket-keeper is not obstructing the view, and is most helpful in assessing how close an lbw decision may be. For a little while I enjoyed this technique, but as time went on I found it to be boring, and if there were not sufficient wide-angle shots punched on the screen then I was inclined to forget who was bowling from which end. Thus the viewer is not able to watch the cricket as a spectator does, and is rather left at the mercy of the director. I missed the variety that our coverage gives and would prefer to see the opposite view restricted to playbacks of any incident of real note.

There are always problems when cricket is covered on commercial television, and to help pay the enormous bills of WSC, commercial breaks occur at the end of just about every over. There are occasions when they overrun the cricket, but more important they have an adverse effect on the commentary. Normally the short interval between overs is at the disposal of the expert summariser but as this time is denied to him, his only recourse is to interrupt constantly the ball by ball describer, and in the end there seemed to be an awful lot of chatter. It is only fair to say that this does not offend the Australian viewing public as much as it would the English, as over the years they have been educated to it on all channels.

What upset me more than anything else was the attitude of the commentators themselves. It may be that I should be the last person to offer this kind of criticism and in doing so I obviously leave myself

Dennis Lillee, who was unfit to tour England in 1977, is now one of Kerry Packer's biggest draws, WSC Australia's answer to the battery of fast bowlers which the West Indians can field.

wide open. One day in Perth I listened attentively for four solid hours to the comments of Richie Benaud and Fred Trueman, followed by Tony Cozier and Keith Stackpole. It was a very ordinary and unexciting contest, yet every scoring shot was described as 'magnificent', every ball that beat the bat was an 'outstanding' delivery, each and every throw-in was 'superb' or 'spot on'. One long throw from Max Walker was quite dreadful, giving Rodney Marsh a ten-yard dash to collect it, yet it was described as 'slightly off target'. All the players in turn were credited as world beaters and never once did I hear a single word of criticism offered of the cricket or the cricketers. Especially after listening to my old friend, Fred Trueman, waxing forth on English radio during

155

the summer, when he does such a first class job without ever pulling any punches, I could only come to the conclusion that on Channel 9 the commentators must be under instructions not to devalue WSC, and as a result much of the commentary did not ring true to me.

Moving from WSC to the official Test matches at Brisbane and Perth gave me a chance to compare the relative strengths of the two Australian sides in action. I could only do this by using the England side as a yardstick. Brearley's side had completely outplayed Australia in 1977, yet Greg Chappell's side began to dominate WSC in 1978-79. If there was no Lillee in England in 1977, there was no Thomson in Australia in 1978-79. The young, raw and inexperienced new Australians under Graham Yallop began to prosper and ultimately beat the Englishmen, who surely had not gone backwards, at Melbourne, and later gave them a hard time at Sydney.

At the same time no one would suggest that either England or Australia had in their ranks batsmen of the class of Greg Chappell, Viv Richards and Clive Lloyd, or bowlers equal to Dennis Lillee, Jeff Thomson and Andy Roberts. Remember however that there are now some 60 cricketers under contract to Kerry Packer, many of whom are either on their way out or who, on the other hand, are unlikely to make the grade. There remains therefore only a select few who are likely to be the draw cards. For how long will the Australian public continue to watch the same players in opposition week in and week out? I would have thought that if WSC is to remain in business for any length of time then they will have to part with the Snows, Holfords, Fredericks, Barlows etc, and try to tempt over the Hoggs, the Gowers, and the Bothams. This of course may now prove difficult, not only for contractual reasons but for financial ones. Kerry Packer would have to think now in terms of three times the amount he pays his present players to tempt further English signings. The Australian Cricket Board seems to be of the opinion that in the end Packer cricket will die because his supply of players will dry up. I would have thought he will always have a ready market in West Indies, Pakistan and South Africa, but more than ever before the Australian crowds have become fiercely partisan and will only attend in large numbers if they believe the home side is on to a 'good thing'.

One vital question to be faced and answered concerns the saturation point of television coverage on cricket. One day in Perth I watched a WSC match being played in Melbourne, pressed a second button to look in at a Gillette Cup game in Brisbane and when I tired of that I pressed a third button and saw NSW v Victoria in a Shield game from Sydney!

For a long time now I have felt sure that some form of compromise between WSC and the various establishments is the

156

WSC cricket. A helmeted Tony Greig lofts a rare boundary for the World XI against the West Indians in a one-day World Series International Cup match at Gloucester Park, Perth, in 1978.

only way to bring cricket back to its traditionally peaceful state. I cannot see Kerry Packer withdrawing from the fight; indeed why should he? Traditional Test cricket will continue and there will not be an ultimate winner. When limited-over or one-day cricket first appeared in England it was opposed by countless thousands, yet it has survived to be both highly successful and financially rewarding to players and clubs alike. As I see it WSC is no different. It could be integrated into our cricket calendar without any real problem and played in various parts of the world. In return it would bring great benefits to spectators, players and international cricket bodies. The conflict between Packer and the authorities changes all the time, and nothing would please me more if when this chapter appears in print, the problem is on its way to being resolved.'

From the Test players' viewpoint, whether they are pro or anti the Australian who turned cricket upside down, they all should give him a vote of thanks. He certainly put a firecracker under the tables at Lord's and Melbourne.

Index

159

Acknowledgements

Associated Newspapers, Sydney: 121 bottom left;
Central Press, London: 10 left, 10 right, 17, 20-21,
22, 23, 24, 30, 31, 43, 48-49, 56, 57, 67 left, 71, 72,
76-77, 90, 92, 94, 95, 101, 103, 105, 109 right, 110
bottom, 113 top, 115 top, 117 bottom right, 119
bottom right, 120 top, 120 bottom, 121 top, 121
bottom right, 123 top, 123 bottom, 125, 127, 134, 136
left, 136 right, 137 left, 137 right, 139, 145, 146, 153,
155, 157; Patrick Eagar: 26, 28-29, 34, 36-37, 40, 44,
45, 46, 47, 50, 51, 52, 53, 54-55, 60, 61, 63, 64-65, 79,
82, 85, 93, 109 left, 110 top, 111 top, 111 bottom, 112
top, 112 bottom, 113 bottom, 114 top, 114 bottom,
115 bottom, 116 top, 117 bottom left, 118 top, 128-
129, 130 left, 130-131, 133, 140-141, 141 Inset, 143,
149; Fox Photos, London: 59; Hamlyn Group
Picture Library: 116 bottom; Mansell Collection,
London: 66, 107; Press Association, London: 11, 39,
84-85, 91, 117 top, 118 bottom, 119 top; Sport &
General Press Agency, London: 12, 32, 33, 38, 67
right, 75, 119 left, 126; Syndication International,
London: 135.

The remaining photographs are from the author's
collection.